ALL IN A ROW AGAIN

23 ROW-BY-ROW QUILT DESIGNS

Compiled by Lissa Alexander

Martingale®
Create with Confidence

Moda All-Stars
All in a Row Again: 23 Row-by-Row Quilt Designs
© 2017 by Martingale & Company®

Martingale®
19021 120th Ave. NE, Ste. 102
Bothell, WA 98011-9511 USA
ShopMartingale.com

Printed in China
22 21 20 19 18 17   8 7 6 5 4 3 2 1

**Library of Congress Cataloging-in-Publication Data
is available upon request.**

ISBN: 978-1-60468-897-9

MISSION STATEMENT

We empower makers who use fabric and yarn
to make life more enjoyable.

CREDITS

**PUBLISHER AND
CHIEF VISIONARY OFFICER**
Jennifer Erbe Keltner

CONTENT DIRECTOR
Karen Costello Soltys

DESIGN MANAGER
Adrienne Smitke

MANAGING EDITOR
Tina Cook

PRODUCTION MANAGER
Regina Girard

ACQUISITIONS EDITOR
Karen M. Burns

PHOTOGRAPHER
Brent Kane

TECHNICAL EDITOR
Elizabeth Beese

ILLUSTRATOR
Sandy Huffaker

COPY EDITOR
Melissa Bryan

TECHNICAL WRITER
Debra Finan

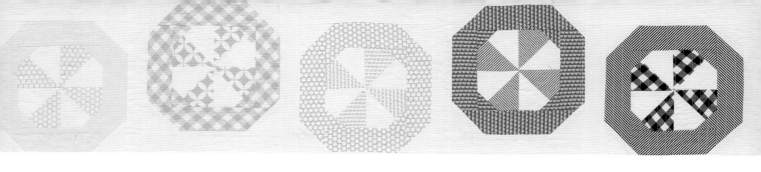

Contents

ALL TOGETHER NOW

Few things are better than getting a group of friends together, unless it's getting them together again. After all, the fun is in the memories we share, the history of what we've done and made, and the anticipation of pleasures ahead.

I'd like to think you have that same anticipation about what follows in these pages. After all, many of you joined in with the first *Moda All-Stars All in a Row* book to create spectacular row quilts and delightful runners. So much so that we had to circle the All-Stars together to round up another heaping helping of stunning rows. You might find even more favorites in this volume. Mix and match them to your heart's content. Or, get out that first book and mix and match rows from both books. The choice is yours! The creativity to make a one-of-a-kind quilt with your signature style and colors is in your hands now.

One thing that hasn't changed—together we're all still making a difference for good! Know that your purchase of this book is helping children with life-threatening illnesses enjoy weeklong, cost-free vacations with their families. Together, the designers are donating royalties from this book's sales to benefit Give Kids the World Village.

Happy together, let's keep rowing along!

~ Lissa Alexander

Springtime

Designed by COREY YODER of Coriander Quilts

FINISHED ROW: 8" × 48"

Use an easy stitch-and-flip method to create colorful posies and verdant green leaves in this springtime row.

Materials

Yardage is based on 42"-wide fabric.

⅝ yard of light print for background
5" × 5" square *each of 13* assorted prints for flowers
5" × 5" square *each of 13* assorted green prints for stems and leaves

Cutting

All measurements include ¼"-wide seam allowances.

From the light print, cut:
1 strip, 3½" × 42"; crosscut into
    7 squares, 3½" × 3½"
1 strip, 2¼" × 42"; crosscut into
    12 squares, 2¼" × 2¼"
1 strip, 2" × 42"; crosscut into
    2 rectangles, 2" × 8½"
1 strip, 1¾" × 42"; crosscut into:
    7 rectangles, 1¾" × 2½"
    14 rectangles, 1" × 1¾"
2 strips, 1½" × 42"; crosscut into
    48 squares, 1½" × 1½"
2 strips, 1¼" × 42"; crosscut into:
    12 rectangles, 1¼" × 2¼"
    24 squares, 1¼" × 1¼"
2 strips, 1" × 42"; crosscut into
    70 squares, 1" × 1"

From *each of 6* prints for flowers, cut:
4 squares, 2½" × 2½" (24 total)

From *each of 7* prints for flowers, cut:
4 squares, 2" × 2" (28 total)

From *each of 6* green prints, cut:
1 rectangle, 1" × 4½" (6 total)
2 rectangles, 2" × 2¼" (12 total)

From *each of 7* green prints, cut:
1 rectangle, 1" × 2½" (7 total)
1 rectangle, 1½" × 1¾" (7 total)

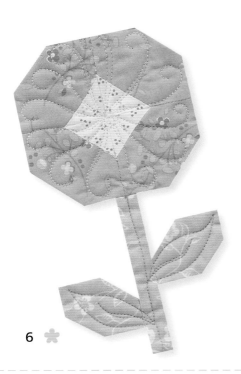

6 ✳

Make the Large Flower Blocks

Press all seam allowances as indicated by the arrows, or as otherwise instructed.

1 Draw a diagonal line from corner to corner on the wrong side of each light 1½" square. Layer two marked squares on opposite corners of a print 2½" square, right sides together as shown. Sew on the marked lines. Trim ¼" from the stitching lines. Press. Repeat to make a total of 24 large flower units.

Make 24 units,
2½" × 2½".

PRESSING SEAM ALLOWANCES

When making the flower units, Corey presses diagonal seam allowances open to reduce bulk.

2 Lay out four matching flower units as shown. Sew the units into two rows. Join the rows to make a large flower top. Repeat to make a total of six large flower tops. Each should be 4½" square.

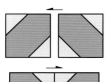

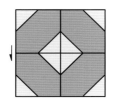

Make 6 units,
4½" × 4½".

3 In the same manner, layer two light 1¼" squares on a green 2" × 2¼" rectangle as shown. Stitch, trim, and press to make a left leaf. Repeat to make a total of six different green left leaves.

Make 6 units,
2" × 2¼".

4 In the same manner, make six green right leaves as shown.

Make 6 units,
2" × 2¼".

5 Sew a light 2¼" square to the top of each left leaf and a light 1¼" × 2¼" rectangle to the bottom.

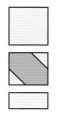 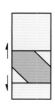

6 Sew a light 1¼" × 2¼" rectangle to the top of each right leaf and a light 2¼" square to the bottom.

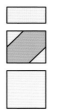

7 Lay out a green 1" × 4½" rectangle with its matching left-hand and right-hand leaf units. Join the pieces to make a large stem unit. Repeat to make a total of six large stem units.

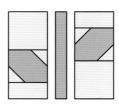 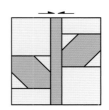

Make 6 units,
4½" × 4½".

8 Join a flower top and a stem unit to make a Large Flower block. The block should measure 4½" × 8½". Repeat to make a total of six Large Flower blocks.

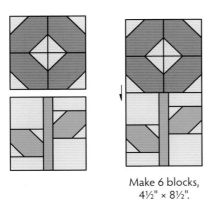

Make 6 blocks, 4½" × 8½".

Make the Small Flower Blocks

1 Draw a diagonal line from corner to corner on the wrong side of each light 1" square. Layer two marked squares on opposite corners of a print 2" square, right sides together as shown. Sew on the marked lines. Trim ¼" from the stitching lines and press to make a small flower unit. Repeat to make seven sets of four matching small flower units.

Make 28 units, 2" × 2".

2 Lay out four matching small flower units as shown. Sew the units into two rows. Join the rows to make a small flower top. Repeat to make a total of seven small flower tops. Each small flower top should measure 3½" square.

Make 7 units, 3½" × 3½".

3 In the same manner, layer two light 1" squares on a green 1½" × 1¾" rectangle. Stitch, trim, and press to make a left leaf. Repeat to make a total of three green left leaves.

Make 3 units, 1½" × 1¾".

4 In the same manner, make four green right leaves as shown.

Make 4 units, 1½" × 1¾".

5 Sew a light 1" × 1¾" rectangle to the top and bottom of each leaf unit as shown.

Make 3 units, 1¾" × 2½".   Make 4 units, 1¾" × 2½".

6 Sew together a left leaf unit, the matching 1" × 2½" green rectangle, and a 1¾" × 2½" light rectangle to make a small stem unit. Press. Repeat to make a total of three small stem units.

Make 3 units, 2½" × 3½".

7 Using right leaf units, repeat step 6 to make four additional small stem units.

Make 4 units, 2½" × 3½".

8 Join each flower top to a stem unit; press. Sew a light 3½" square to the top to make a Small Flower block; press. The block should measure 3½" × 8½". Repeat to make a total of seven Small Flower blocks.

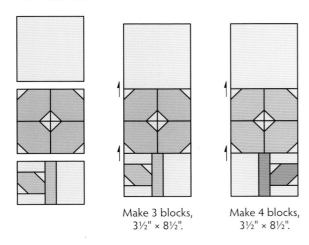

Make 3 blocks,
3½" × 8½".

Make 4 blocks,
3½" × 8½".

Assemble the Row

Referring to the photo on page 6, lay out the Small Flower and Large Flower blocks in alternating positions. Join the blocks. Sew a light 2" × 8½" strip to each end of the row. The completed row should measure 8½" × 48½", including seam allowances.

HERE'S THE SKINNY ON
COREY YODER

She's got a signature style that's all her own as Little Miss Shabby (CorianderQuilts.com). Find out a little bit more about how she gets the look she loves.

I'm currently obsessed with pretty sticky notes, stationery, and pens.

I'd line up every time to hang out with my friends—I have some great ones!

My go-to sewing thread color is white. I use it for 95% of my piecing.

The most productive time of day for me to sew is 1:00 to 3:00 p.m.

My favorite marking tool is a Dritz Mark-B-Gone. I use it almost any time a marking tool is needed!

The last great series I binge-watched was *Canada's Worst Driver.* It was a hoot!

My go-to rotary cutter is a 60 mm.

My go-to scissors are Fiskars 8" shears.

When pulling fabric for a single row like this, I begin by choosing a color palette and then raiding my scrap bin.

One little tip that will make creating my row better is to choose a fun background fabric—it adds pizzazz.

Pollen

Designed by **JEN KINGWELL**

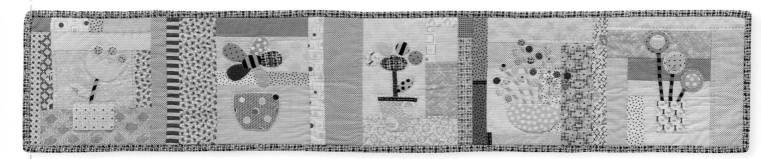

FINISHED ROW: 9" × 48"

These cute little pots of blooms are easy to make using the appliqué method of your choice and lots of your favorite bits of fabric.

Materials

Yardage is based on 42"-wide fabric.

¾ yard *total* of gray prints for background
Assorted scraps of bright prints for appliqué and spacers

Cutting

All measurements include ¼"-wide seam allowances.

From the assorted gray prints, cut:
5 rectangles and/or squares, assorted sizes for block centers (see the block layouts on pages 11 and 12 for ideas)
Assorted-width strips, 1¼" to 3½" wide × up to 11" long

From the assorted bright prints, cut:
4 strips, 1¼" × 9½", for spacers between blocks

ADD VARIETY
Add a few bright print strips for fun and interest if desired.

Assemble and Appliqué the Blocks

Starting with a gray square or rectangle for the center, and cutting gray strips of various widths as you go, randomly add strips to make a block approximately 11" × 11" as shown in the following examples. Press the seam allowances toward each strip as you add it. Repeat to make a total of five blocks.

1 Block A appears on the left end of the quilt. To make the block as shown in the quilt, cut assorted gray pieces in the dimensions shown below. Assemble the block center in a counterclockwise Log Cabin style. Then join the smaller rectangles together side by side and add them to the top of the block. Finally, add long rectangles to the left and right of the block. Press.

3 To make block C, join the smaller rectangles as shown in a clockwise Log Cabin fashion. Sew this unit to the right edge of a 4¾" × 8¼" rectangle. Join a 3¼" × 7¾" rectangle to the bottom of the unit. Complete the block by sewing a 3¾" × 11" strip to the left edge of the unit. Press.

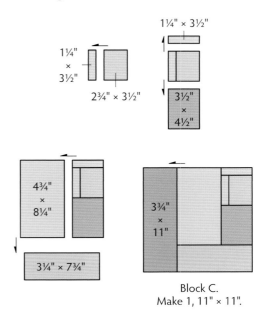

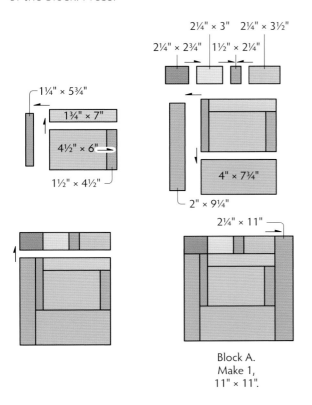

Block C.
Make 1, 11" × 11".

4 Block D is also made Log Cabin style. Sew the smaller rectangles around a 4½" × 5" center piece. Join the larger pieces around the center. Press.

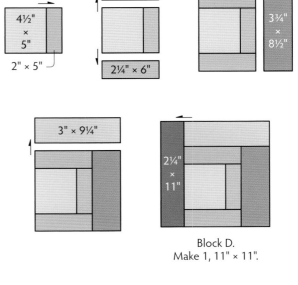

Block A.
Make 1,
11" × 11".

2 Block B is simply made of four rectangles joined along their long edges to make a stack. Finish by adding a 3¾" × 11" rectangle to the left edge of the block. Press.

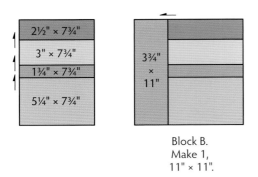

Block B.
Make 1,
11" × 11".

Block D.
Make 1, 11" × 11".

HERE'S THE SKINNY ON
JEN KINGWELL

Learn a bit more about the Aussie wonder down under at the helm of Jen Kingwell Designs (JenKingwellDesigns.blogspot.com).

I'm currently obsessed with my acrylic templates. I love using them.

I'd line up every time to eat good ice cream, especially salted caramel.

My go-to sewing thread color is 50-weight Aurifil #6725 (a light taupe). I use it for 90% of my piecing.

The most productive time of day for me to sew is 8:00 to 10:00 a.m.

My favorite marking tool is a hera marker. I use it for marking quilting lines.

The last great series I binge-watched was *The Real Housewives of Beverly Hills.*

My go-to rotary cutter is a 45 mm.

My go-to scissors are 5" Kai scissors.

When pulling fabric for a single row like this, I begin by gathering lots of fabrics, and then I choose which ones to use.

One little tip that will make creating my row better is: Don't fuss too much about placement. It's a free and easy design.

5 Block E looks more like a Quarter Log Cabin, with rectangles or strips being added to just two adjacent sides of the center piece. To complete the block, add a 3¼" × 9¼" strip to the right of the unit, and then sew a 2¼" × 11" strip to the top of the unit. Press.

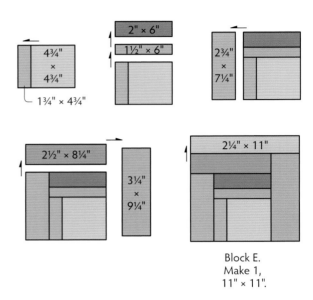

Block E.
Make 1,
11" × 11".

6 Using the patterns on pages 13–15, prepare the shapes for appliqué. Jen used turned-edge appliqué. For more information on this technique, go to ShopMartingale.com/HowtoQuilt. Or, if you prefer, you can use fusible appliqué (you'll need to reverse the patterns). Position and appliqué the prepared shapes on each pieced block, referring to the photo on page 10. Trim each block to 9½" square.

Assemble the Row

Lay out the blocks and bright 1¼" × 9½" strips in alternating positions. Jen's blocks appear in order from A to E, but you can place yours in whatever order you like best.

Join the blocks and strips into a row and press the seam allowances toward the bright strips. The completed row should measure 9½" × 48½", including seam allowances.

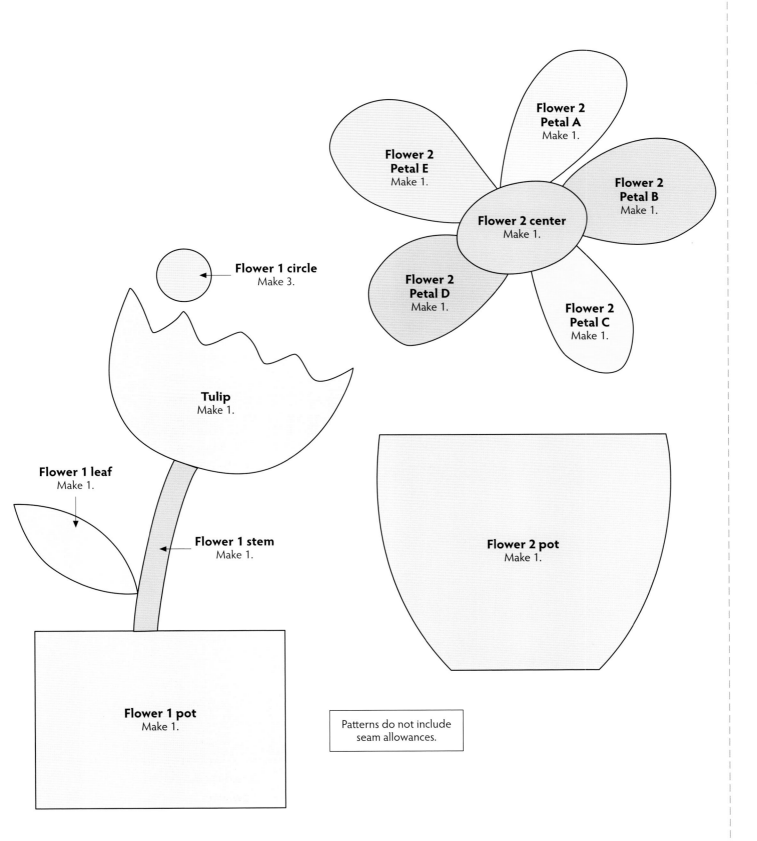

Flower 2 Petal A
Make 1.

Flower 2 Petal E
Make 1.

Flower 2 Petal B
Make 1.

Flower 2 center
Make 1.

Flower 2 Petal D
Make 1.

Flower 2 Petal C
Make 1.

Flower 1 circle
Make 3.

Tulip
Make 1.

Flower 1 leaf
Make 1.

Flower 1 stem
Make 1.

Flower 2 pot
Make 1.

Flower 1 pot
Make 1.

Patterns do not include seam allowances.

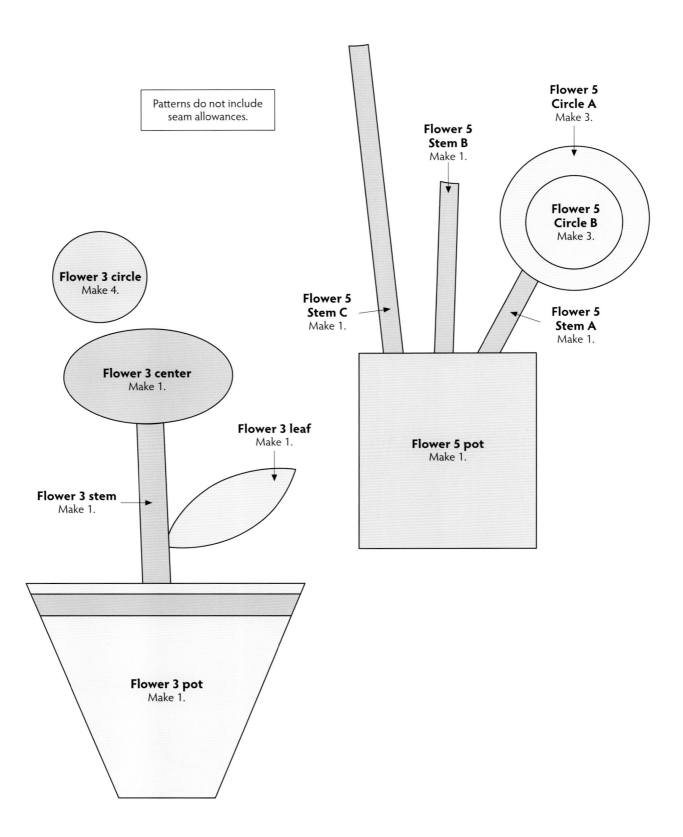

Patterns do not include seam allowances.

Flower 5 Stem B
Make 1.

Flower 5 Circle A
Make 3.

Flower 5 Circle B
Make 3.

Flower 5 Stem C
Make 1.

Flower 5 Stem A
Make 1.

Flower 3 circle
Make 4.

Flower 3 center
Make 1.

Flower 3 leaf
Make 1.

Flower 3 stem
Make 1.

Flower 5 pot
Make 1.

Flower 3 pot
Make 1.

Patterns do not include
seam allowances.

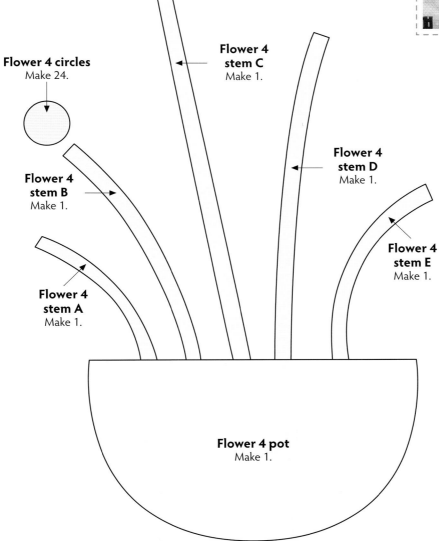

Flower 4 circles
Make 24.

**Flower 4
stem C**
Make 1.

**Flower 4
stem D**
Make 1.

**Flower 4
stem B**
Make 1.

**Flower 4
stem E**
Make 1.

**Flower 4
stem A**
Make 1.

Flower 4 pot
Make 1.

Gone Camping

Designed by **PAT SLOAN**

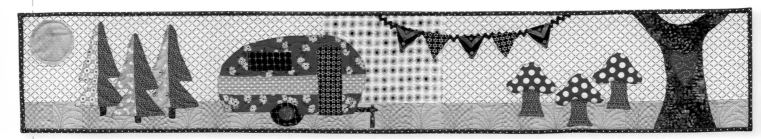

FINISHED ROW: 8" × 48"

Fabric selection is key to creating a nostalgic mood for this camping scene. Combine polka dots, plaids, and florals for a fun retro look.

Materials

Fat quarters are 18" × 21". Fat eighths are 9" × 21".

1 fat quarter of light print A for sky

10" × 10" square of light print B for sky

2 fat eighths of chartreuse prints for grass

1 fat eighth of red print for camper appliqué

2" × 11" rectangle of tan print for camper stripe appliqué

10" × 10" square of dark green print for pine tree and mushroom stem appliqués

5" × 5" square *each of 3* light green prints for pine tree appliqués

4" × 4" square of light blue print for moon appliqué

Scraps of assorted dark blue prints for flag, camper door, window, and tire appliqués

10" × 10" square of brown print for trunk, tree, and trailer hitch appliqués

3" × 3" square of red print for heart and hubcap appliqués

4" × 8" rectangle of red polka dot for mushroom cap appliqués

15" length of dark blue ½"-wide rickrack

¾ yard of 17"-wide lightweight paper-backed fusible web

Basting glue

Cutting

All measurements include ¼"-wide seam allowances.

From light print A, cut:
2 rectangles, 6½" × 20½"

From light print B, cut:
1 rectangle, 6½" × 8½"

From *each of the 2* chartreuse prints, cut:
12 squares, 2½" × 2½" (24 total)

Assemble the Background

1 Sew a light print A rectangle to each 6½" side of the light print B rectangle to make the sky unit. Press the seam allowances in one direction.

2 Lay out the chartreuse squares, alternating the prints. Sew the squares side by side to make the grass unit. Press the seam allowances in one direction, opposite to the direction used for the sky unit.

3 Sew the sky and grass units together. Press the seam allowances toward the sky unit. The completed row should measure 8½" × 48½", including seam allowances.

Appliqué the Row

For information on appliqué and embroidery techniques, go to ShopMartingale.com/HowtoQuilt.

1 Referring to the photo on page 16 as needed, position the rickrack on the pieced background. Adhere the rickrack with a line of basting glue, and then stitch in place with a straight stitch.

2 Using the patterns on pages 18 and 19, prepare the shapes for fusible appliqué. Arrange the shapes on the pieced background. Follow the manufacturer's instructions to fuse the shapes in place. Stitch around each appliqué using a zigzag stitch, blanket stitch, or stitch of your choice to permanently attach the shapes to the background.

HERE'S THE SKINNY ON
PAT SLOAN

She's a social (media) butterfly who's never met a quilter that wasn't soon a friend. Catch a glimpse of what she's into now (PatSloan.com).

I'm currently obsessed with tools to make quilting better—rulers, pins, gadgets. I'm trying out new things.

I'd line up every time for a cup of coffee when I really need it.

My go-to sewing thread color is all the colors in my Aurifil Perfect Box of Neutrals—taupe, grays, and browns. I use it for 99% of my piecing.

The most productive time of day for me to sew is 4:00 to 6:00 p.m. (which I rarely get to do).

My favorite marking tool is my laser guide on my Baby Lock Destiny II. I use it when I'm sewing half-square triangles.

The last great series I binge-watched was *House Hunters International.* Having lived in Europe for eight years, I love seeing other countries!

My go-to rotary cutter is a 45 mm.

My go-to scissors are Havel's 8" shears.

When pulling fabric for a single row like this, I begin by looking at the largest element, the fabric for the caravan. Then I decide whether we are camping during the day or at night, so the background is the second decision.

One little tip that will make creating my row better is: Draw a liquid basting glue line then place the rickrack for the banner on top of it.

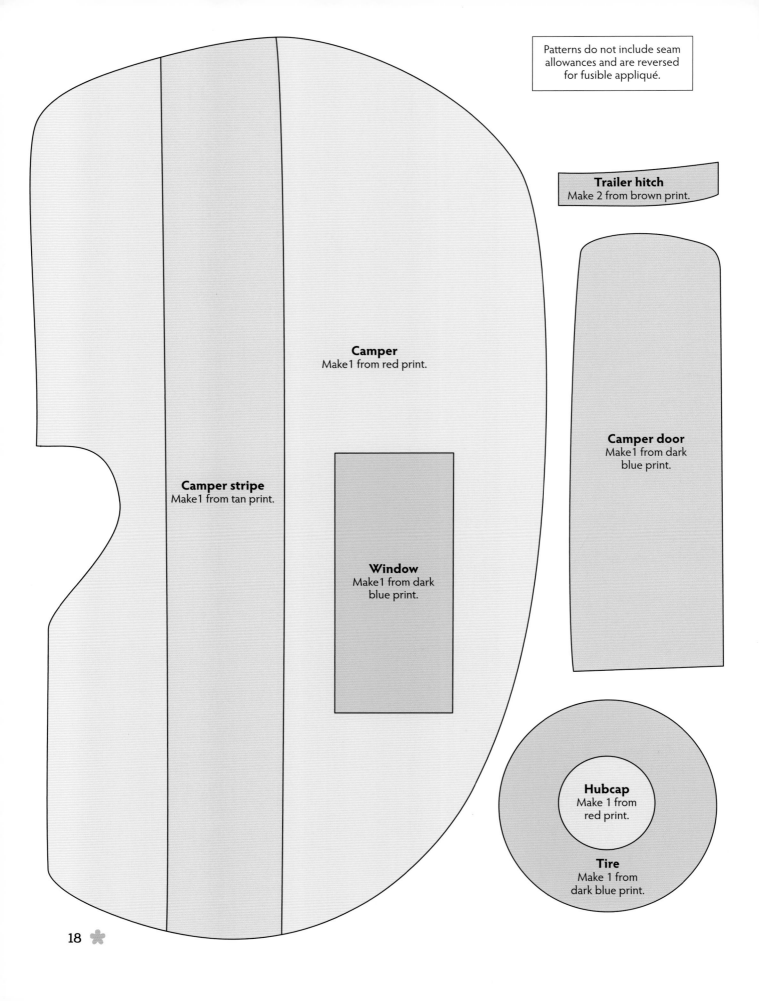

Patterns do not include seam allowances and are reversed for fusible appliqué.

Trailer hitch
Make 2 from brown print.

Camper
Make 1 from red print.

Camper door
Make 1 from dark blue print.

Camper stripe
Make 1 from tan print.

Window
Make 1 from dark blue print.

Hubcap
Make 1 from red print.

Tire
Make 1 from dark blue print.

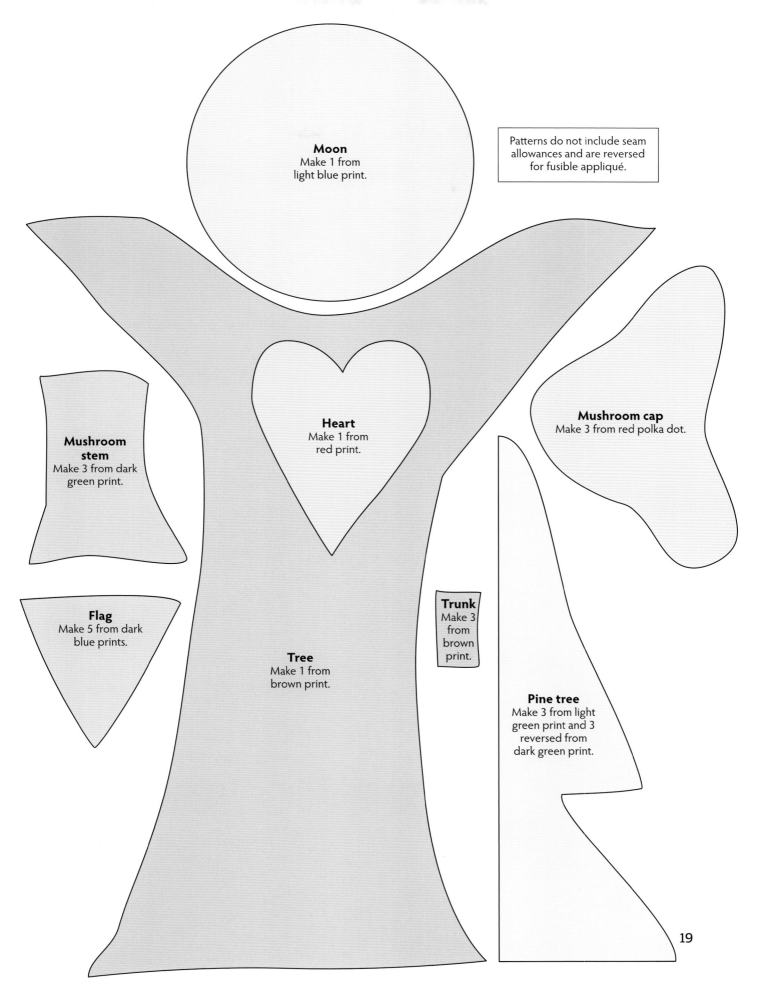

Moon
Make 1 from
light blue print.

Patterns do not include seam
allowances and are reversed
for fusible appliqué.

Mushroom stem
Make 3 from dark
green print.

Heart
Make 1 from
red print.

Mushroom cap
Make 3 from red polka dot.

Flag
Make 5 from dark
blue prints.

Trunk
Make 3
from
brown
print.

Tree
Make 1 from
brown print.

Pine tree
Make 3 from light
green print and 3
reversed from
dark green print.

Oak Silhouettes

Designed by **JANET CLARE**

FINISHED ROW: 8" × 48"

Huge oak trees in a garden were the inspiration for this row. Fusible web and machine appliqué make quick work of the blocks.

Materials

Yardage is based on 42"-wide fabric.

4 squares, 2½" × 2½", *each* of black, dark gray, light gray, and cream prints for sashing
¼ yard of navy mottled print for tree appliqués
⅝ yard of green print for background
¼ yard of 17"-wide lightweight paper-backed fusible web

Cutting

All measurements include ¼"-wide seam allowances.

From the green print, cut:
5 squares, 8½" × 8½"

Make the Sashing

Sew together one black square, one dark gray square, one light gray square, and one cream square in a row to make a sashing unit. Press the seam allowances in one direction. Repeat to make a total of four sashing units, placing the squares randomly in each.

Make 4 units, 2½" × 8½", changing the fabric placement in each unit.

Make the Tree Blocks

Using the tree pattern below, prepare five navy trees for fusible appliqué. For illustrated information on fusible appliqué, go to ShopMartingale.com/HowtoQuilt. Referring to the photo on page 20 as needed, center one tree on each green background square. Follow the manufacturer's instructions to fuse the trees in place. Stitch around each appliqué using a zigzag stitch, blanket stitch, or stitch of your choice to permanently attach the trees to the squares.

Assemble the Row

Sew the Tree blocks and sashing units together in alternating positions. Press the seam allowances toward the blocks. The completed row should measure 8½" × 48½", including seam allowances.

Tree
Make 5 from navy
mottled print.

Pattern does not include seam allowances and is reversed for fusible appliqué.

Summer Blooms

Designed by **LAURIE SIMPSON** of Minick and Simpson

FINISHED ROW: 10" × 48"

These scrappy appliqué lollipop flowers couldn't be easier . . . or cuter! The red, white, and blue prints bring to mind a hot, lazy day in July.

Materials

Yardage is based on 42"-wide fabric.

1½ yards of cream print for background
10" × 10" square *each of 2* dark blue prints for stem, leaf, and flower appliqués
Scraps of red and blue prints, stripes, and plaids for flower appliqués
Clover bias tape maker (6 mm)
Basting glue

Cutting

All measurements include ¼"-wide seam allowances.

From the *lengthwise grain* of the cream print, cut:
1 strip, 10½" × 48½"

Appliqué the Row

1 Using the bias tape maker, cut and prepare nine ¼" × 6" lengths of bias tape from dark blue prints for the stems.

2 Using the patterns on pages 23 and 24, prepare the shapes for turned-edge appliqué. For more information on turned-edge appliqué, go to ShopMartingale.com/HowtoQuilt.

3 Referring to the photo above as a guide, arrange and appliqué the stems, leaves, and flowers on the background rectangle. Stems should be placed about 4¾" apart. The completed row should measure 10½" × 48½", including seam allowances.

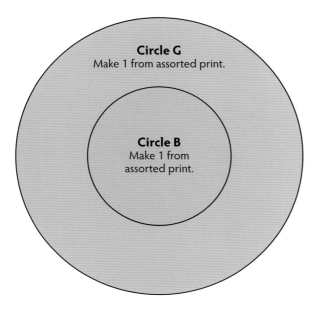

Circle G
Make 1 from assorted print.

Circle B
Make 1 from assorted print.

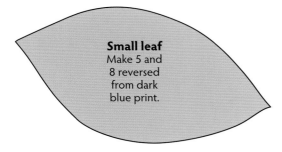

Small leaf
Make 5 and 8 reversed from dark blue print.

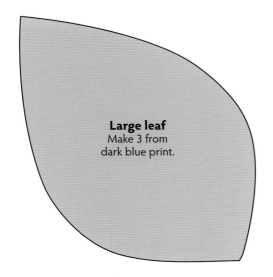

Large leaf
Make 3 from dark blue print.

Patterns do not include seam allowances.

Circle K
Make 1 from assorted print.

Circle H
Make 2 from assorted prints.

Circle A
Make 4 from assorted prints.

Circle E
Make 1 from assorted print.

Circle I
Make 1 from assorted print.

Circle F
Make 1 from assorted print.

Circle C
Make 3 from assorted prints.

Circle J
Make 1 from dark blue print and 1 from assorted print.

Circle D
Make 1 from assorted print.

Patterns do not include seam allowances.

Garden Time

Designed by LYNNE HAGMEIER of Kansas Troubles Quilters

FINISHED ROW: 10" × 48"

Raw-edge appliqué adds a rustic look to this row of posies.

Materials

Yardage is based on 42"-wide fabric. Fat quarters are 18" × 21". Fat eighths are 9" × 21".

⅔ yard of tan print for background

5" × 5" square *each of 8* prints (2 red, 2 navy, 2 gold, 2 purple) for petals

2½" × 2½" square *each of 8* prints (2 red, 2 navy, 2 gold, 2 purple) for flower centers

1 fat quarter of green print for leaf and stem appliqués and checkerboard

1 fat eighth of black print for watering can appliqués

⅓ yard of 17"-wide lightweight paper-backed fusible web

Basting glue

Cutting

All measurements include ¼"-wide seam allowances.

From *each of the 8* prints for petals, cut:
4 squares, 2½" × 2½" (32 total)

From *each of the 8* prints for flower centers, cut *on the bias*:
1 square, 1" × 1" (8 total)

From the green print, cut:
3 strips, 1½" × 21"
4 squares, 1½" × 1½"

Continued on page 26

Continued from page 25

From the black print, cut:

1 rectangle, 5½" × 6½"

From the tan print, cut:

2 strips, 4½" × 42"; crosscut into:

    1 rectangle, 4½" × 5½"

    8 rectangles, 3½" × 4½"

    4 rectangles, 2½" × 4½"

    4 rectangles, 1½" × 4½"

1 rectangle, 2½" × 8½"

4 strips, 1½" × 42"; crosscut into:

    3 strips, 1½" × 21"

    4 strips, 1½" × 9½"

    5 strips, 1½" × 8½"

2 strips, 1¼" × 42"; crosscut into 48 squares, 1¼" × 1¼". Cut the squares in half diagonally to yield 96 triangles.

Make the Flower Blocks

Press all seam allowances as indicated by the arrows, or as otherwise instructed.

1 Layer a tan triangle, right side up, on each of three corners of a 2½" petal square. Glue-baste the triangle in place. Using matching tan thread, topstitch ⅛" from the long edge of each triangle as shown. Repeat to make four matching petal squares.

Make 4 units,
2½" × 2½".

2 Sew the petals together in two rows of two. Join the rows to make a flower unit, 4½" square.

Make 1 unit,
4½" × 4½".

3 Repeat steps 1 and 2 to make a total of eight flower units.

4 Center a contrasting print 1" bias square on each flower unit as shown. Glue-baste the squares in place. Using black thread, topstitch ⅛" from the edges of each square and stitch an X across each square.

- -

BIAS IS BETTER

While quilters usually avoid bias, it works best for this type of raw-edge appliqué because fabrics cut on the bias won't fray or ravel.

- -

5 Matching 4½" edges, sew a tan 1½" × 4½" rectangle to the top of a purple flower unit and a tan 3½" × 4½" rectangle to the bottom to make a Short Flower block. Repeat for the second purple flower, one red flower, and one gold flower.

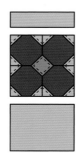
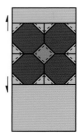

Make 2 blocks,
4½" × 8½".

Make 1 block,
4½" × 8½".

Make 1 block,
4½" × 8½".

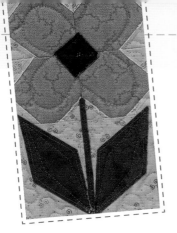

6 Sew a tan 2½" × 4½" rectangle to the top of a gold flower and a tan 3½" × 4½" rectangle to the bottom to make a Tall Flower block. Repeat for two blue flowers and one red flower.

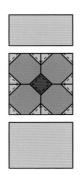
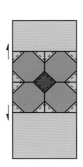

Make 1 block,
4½" × 9½".

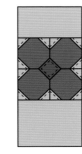

Make 2 blocks,
4½" × 9½".

Make 1 block,
4½" × 9½".

Make the Checkerboard Units

1 Sew two green strips and two tan 1½" × 21" strips together, alternating colors, to make a strip set. Crosscut the strip set into 12 segments, 1½" wide.

1½"

Make 1 strip set.
Cut 12 segments.

2 Sew together one green and one tan 1½" × 21" strip to make a strip set. Crosscut the strip set into seven segments, 1½" wide.

1½"

Make 1 strip set.
Cut 7 segments.

3 Join segments to make checkerboard units as shown. Save the remaining segments for row assembly.

Make 4 units,
2½" × 4½".

Make 1 unit,
2½" × 2½".

Assemble the Row

1 Sew the checkerboard units, green squares, and remaining strip-set segments to the Flower blocks, remaining tan strips, and tan 2½" × 8½" rectangle as shown.

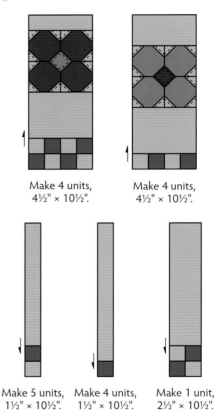

Make 4 units, 4½" × 10½".

Make 4 units, 4½" × 10½".

Make 5 units, 1½" × 10½".

Make 4 units, 1½" × 10½".

Make 1 unit, 2½" × 10½".

2 Sew the tan 4½" × 5½" rectangle to the black rectangle as shown.

Make 1 unit, 5½" × 10½".

3 Join the units from steps 1 and 2 into a row as shown. The completed row should measure 10½" × 48½", including seam allowances.

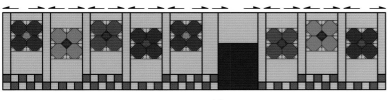

Row assembly

Appliqué the Row

1 Using the patterns below, prepare the shapes for fusible appliqué. For illustrated information on fusible appliqué, go to ShopMartingale.com/HowtoQuilt.

2 Adhere fusible web to the wrong side of a green 2½" × 4½" rectangle. From it, cut eight ¼" × 4" stems.

3 Referring to the photo on page 25, arrange the leaves, stems, and watering can pieces on the background. Follow the manufacturer's instructions to fuse the shapes in place.

4 Stitch around each appliqué using a zigzag stitch, blanket stitch, or stitch of your choice to permanently attach the shapes to the background. Lynne used a straight stitch around each shape.

Patterns do not include seam allowances and are reversed for fusible appliqué.

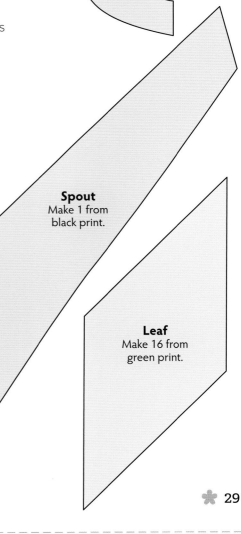

Handle
Make 1 from black print.

Spout
Make 1 from black print.

Top 1
Make 1 from black print.

Sprinkler
Make 1 from black print.

Top 2
Make 1 from black print.

Leaf
Make 16 from green print.

Flitter Flutter

Designed by **STACY IEST HSU**

FINISHED ROW: 7½" × 48"

No springtime quilt is complete without butterflies and tulips! Use an assortment of bright prints for this fresh-as-a-breeze row.

Materials

Yardage is based on 42"-wide fabric.

½ yard *total* of assorted bright prints for butterflies and tulips

½ yard of light print for background

5" × 5" square *each of 6* assorted green prints for stems and leaves

Cutting

All measurements include ¼"-wide seam allowances. Designer Stacy Iest Hsu played around with the color placement in her Butterfly blocks to make a variety of different-looking butterflies. Before cutting bright prints, study Stacy's color placement and read the construction steps to determine if you want to cut matching sets of pieces for the 4" squares and 2½" squares.

From *each of 6* bright prints, cut for tulips:
1 square, 2½" × 2½" (6 total)
1 rectangle, 2" × 3½" (6 total)

From the remainder of the assorted bright prints, cut a *total* of:
8 squares, 4" × 4"
20 squares, 2½" × 2½"

From *each of the 6* green prints, cut:
2 rectangles, 1¾" × 3½" (12 total)
1 rectangle, 1" × 3½" (6 total)

From the light print, cut:
2 strips, 2½" × 42"; crosscut into 26 squares, 2½" × 2½"
2 strips, 1¾" × 42"; crosscut into 24 squares, 1¾" × 1¾"
5 strips, 1¼" × 42"; crosscut *2 of the strips* into 8 strips, 1¼" × 6½", and 12 squares, 1¼" × 1¼"

Make the Butterfly Blocks

Press all seam allowances as indicated by the arrows, or as otherwise instructed.

1. Draw a diagonal line from corner to corner on the wrong side of each light 2½" square, 1¾" square, and 1¼" square; four bright 4" squares; and four bright 2½" squares.

2. Layer a marked bright 2½" square on an unmarked bright 2½" square, right sides together. Stitch ¼" from both sides of the marked line. Cut the squares on the line to make two bright half-square-triangle units. Press the seam allowances toward the darker print. Repeat with three light squares and three bright squares to make six light/bright half-square-triangle units. Press. Trim each unit to 2" square.

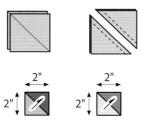

Make 2 units.   Make 6 units.

3. Lay out the half-square-triangle units as shown. (Stacy arranged her triangle units in two different orientations for her blocks.) Sew the units together in each row. Join the rows to make a bottom section.

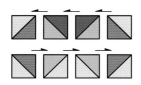 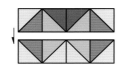

Make 1 unit,
3½" × 6½".

4. Repeat steps 2 and 3 to make a total of four bottom sections.

5. Layer a marked bright 4" square on an unmarked different-colored bright 4" square, right sides together. Stitch, cut, and press as before to make two bright half-square-triangle units. Trim each unit to 3½" square.

Make 2 units.

6. Layer a marked light 2½" square on a half-square-triangle unit as shown. Stitch on the line. Trim ¼" from the stitching line. Repeat to make a mirror-image wing unit.

Make a mirror-image pair,
3½" × 3½".

7. Repeat steps 5 and 6 to make four pairs of wing units.

8. Lay out two wing units and one bottom section as shown. Join the wing units. Join the top and bottom sections to make a block. The block should measure 6½" square. Repeat to make a total of four Butterfly blocks.

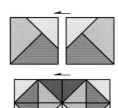 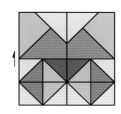

Make 4 blocks,
6½" × 6½".

Make the Tulip Blocks

1 Layer a remaining marked light 2½" square on a bright 2½" square, right sides together. Stitch, cut, and press as before to make two half-square-triangle units. Repeat with the remaining marked light 2½" squares to make 12 light/bright half-square-triangle units. Press the seam allowances toward the bright prints. Trim each unit to 2" square.

Make 12 units.

2 Join two matching half-square-triangle units to make a flower top unit. Press. Repeat to make a total of six flower top units.

Make 6 units, 3½" × 2".

3 Layer two marked light 1¼" squares on a bright rectangle as shown, right sides together. Stitch on the lines. Trim ¼" from the stitching lines. Repeat to make a total of six middle units.

Make 6 units, 3½" × 2".

4 Layer two marked light 1¾" squares on a green 1¾" × 3½" rectangle as shown, right sides together. Stitch, cut, and press as before to make a leaf unit. Make a mirror-image leaf unit using the matching green 1¾" × 3½" rectangle. Repeat to make six matching pairs of leaf units.

Make 6 pairs of units (12 total), 1¾" × 3½".

5 Join the leaf units and matching green 1" × 3½" rectangle to make a flower bottom unit. The unit should measure 3½" square. Repeat to make a total of six flower bottom units.

Make 6 units,
3½" × 3½".

6 Join a flower top unit, matching middle unit, and one flower bottom unit to make a tulip unit as shown. Repeat to make a total of six tulip units.

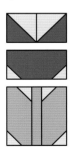 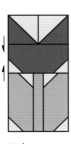

Make 6 units,
3½" × 6½".

7 Join two tulip units to make a Tulip block. The block should measure 6½" square. Repeat to make a total of three Tulip blocks.

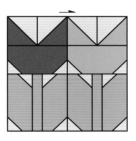

Make 3 blocks,
6½" × 6½".

Assemble the Row

1 Referring to the photo on page 30, lay out the blocks and light 1¼" × 6½" strips in alternating positions. Join the blocks and strips into a row. Press the seam allowances toward the strips.

2 Sew the remaining light 1¼" × 42" strips together end to end. Cut two 48½" lengths from the pieced strip. Sew the strips to the top and bottom of the row. Press the seam allowances toward the strips. The completed row should measure 8" × 48½", including seam allowances.

Hedgehog Run

Designed by ANNE SUTTON of Bunny Hill Designs

FINISHED ROW: 10" × 48"

These lovable critters will surely make you smile!

Materials

Yardage is based on 42"-wide fabric. Fat quarters are 18" × 21". Fat eighths are 9" × 21".

1 fat quarter of cream-and-white dot for background

10" × 10" square *each of 3* pink prints (A, B, and C) for Star blocks and leaf and flower appliqués

4" × 8" rectangle of brown plaid for background

10" × 10" square of beige print for background

1 fat eighth of brown dot for ground, side borders, and flower center appliqués

1 fat quarter of cream-and-tan dot for background

1 fat eighth of brown floral for ground

10" × 10" square of brown stripe for mushroom stem, flower stem, and jump rope appliqués

5" × 5" square of tan print for hedgehog ear and body appliqués

5" × 5" square of pink plaid for hedgehog ear and body appliqués

10" × 10" square of dark brown print for hedgehog fur appliqués

5" × 5" square of medium brown polka dot for mushroom cap appliqués

Clover bias tape maker (6 mm/¼")

Basting glue

Brown embroidery floss

Size 26 hand-embroidery needle

Cutting

All measurements include ¼"-wide seam allowances.

From the cream-and-white dot, cut:
2 rectangles, 5½" × 11½"
1 rectangle, 3½" × 5½"
1 square, 3½" × 3½"
1 rectangle, 3½" × 2½"
6 squares, 2¼" × 2¼"
12 squares, 1½" × 1½"

From pink print A, cut:
6 squares, 2¼" × 2¼"
3 squares, 1½" × 1½"

From the brown plaid, cut:
2 squares, 3½" × 3½"

From the beige print, cut:
1 rectangle, 3½" × 8½"
1 rectangle, 3½" × 5½"

From the brown dot, cut:
2 strips, 2½" × 21"; crosscut into:
   1 rectangle, 2½" × 8½"
   2 rectangles, 2½" × 6½"
2 rectangles, 1½" × 8½"

From the cream-and-tan dot, cut:
1 rectangle, 8½" × 18½"

From the brown floral, cut:
2 strips, 2½" × 21"; crosscut into:
   2 rectangles, 2½" × 8½"
   2 rectangles, 2½" × 6½"

Make the Blocks

Press all seam allowances as indicated by the arrows, or as otherwise instructed.

1 Draw a diagonal line from corner to corner on the wrong side of each cream-and-white 2¼" square. Layer a marked square on a pink 2¼" square, right sides together. Sew ¼" from the line on both sides as shown. Cut on the marked line to make two half-square-triangle units. Repeat to make a total of 12 half-square-triangle units. Trim each unit to 1½" square.

Make 12 units.

2 Lay out four half-square-triangle units, a pink 1½" square, and four cream-and-white 1½" squares as shown. Sew the pieces together in each row. Join the rows to make a Star block. Repeat to make a total of three Star blocks.

Make 3 blocks, 3½" × 3½".

Assemble the Background

1 Lay out one cream-and-white 5½" × 11½" rectangle, one brown plaid square, the beige 3½" × 8½" rectangle, and one brown dot 1½" × 8½" rectangle as shown. Join the pieces to make the left background, which should measure 8½" × 12½".

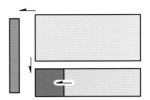

Make 1 left background, 8½" × 12½".

2 Lay out one cream-and-white 5½" × 11½" rectangle, one Star block, the beige 3½" × 5½" rectangle, one brown plaid square, and one brown dot 1½" × 8½" rectangle as shown. Join the pieces to make the right background, which should measure 8½" × 12½".

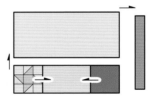

Make 1 right background, 8½" × 12½".

3 Lay out the cream-and-tan rectangle; two Star blocks; and the cream-and-white 3½" × 5½" rectangle, 3½" square, and 2½" × 3½" rectangle as shown. Join the pieces to make the center background. The center background should measure 8½" × 24½".

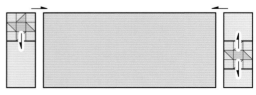

Make 1 center background, 8½" × 24½".

4 Lay out four brown floral rectangles and remaining brown dot rectangles as shown. Sew the rectangles together to make the ground unit. Join the side backgrounds, center background, and ground unit to make the row background. The completed row should measure 10½" × 48½", including seam allowances.

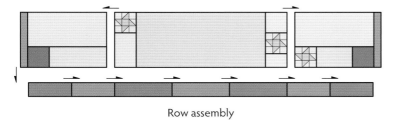

Row assembly

Appliqué the Row

For additional information on appliqué and embroidery techniques, go to ShopMartingale.com/HowtoQuilt.

1 Using the bias tape maker and the square of brown stripe, make one 13" length of ¼"-wide bias tape for the jump rope and two 5½" lengths for the flower stems.

2 Using the patterns on page 38, prepare the shapes for turned-edge appliqué. (If you prefer fusible appliqué, you'll need to reverse the patterns.) Position the prepared shapes on the row background, referring to the photo on page 34 as needed. Use basting glue to hold the jump rope and flower stems in place. Appliqué each piece in place.

3 Embroider eyes and noses using three strands of brown embroidery floss and a satin stitch.

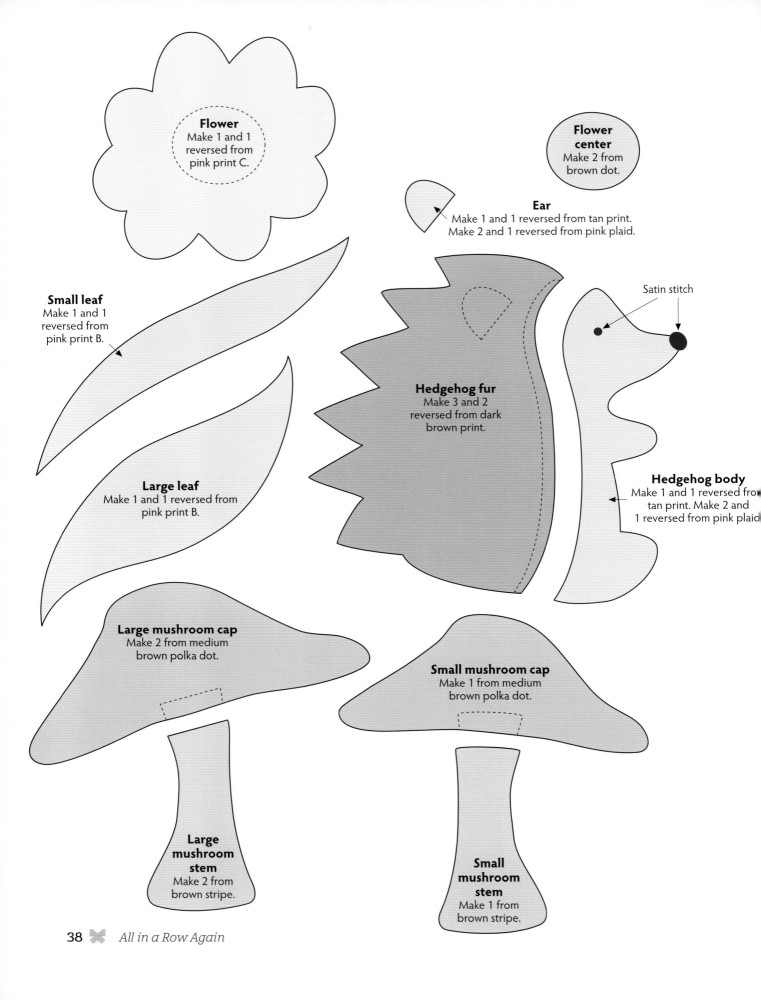

Flower
Make 1 and 1
reversed from
pink print C.

Flower center
Make 2 from
brown dot.

Ear
Make 1 and 1 reversed from tan print.
Make 2 and 1 reversed from pink plaid.

Small leaf
Make 1 and 1
reversed from
pink print B.

Hedgehog fur
Make 3 and 2
reversed from dark
brown print.

Satin stitch

Hedgehog body
Make 1 and 1 reversed from
tan print. Make 2 and
1 reversed from pink plaid.

Large leaf
Make 1 and 1 reversed from
pink print B.

Large mushroom cap
Make 2 from medium
brown polka dot.

Small mushroom cap
Make 1 from medium
brown polka dot.

Large mushroom stem
Make 2 from
brown stripe.

Small mushroom stem
Make 1 from
brown stripe.

Midnight in the Woods

Designed by **ALMA ALLEN of Blackbird Designs**

FINISHED ROW: 8" × 48"

While looking at this row, it's easy to imagine being outside on a quiet, dark night, listening to owls and other creatures in the wild.

Materials

Yardage is based on 42"-wide fabric. Fat quarters are 18" × 21". Fat eighths are 9" × 21".

1 fat quarter *each of 2* black prints for owl backgrounds, eyes, and Star blocks

1 fat eighth of black print for Star blocks

1 fat eighth *each of 3* cheddar prints for Star blocks and moon appliqués

1 fat eighth of purple print for Star blocks and leaf appliqués

1 fat eighth *each of 3* brown prints for Star blocks and owl appliqués

1 fat eighth of green print for stems and leaf appliqués

Scrap of brown solid for feet appliqués

Scrap of light print for face appliqués

Scrap of orange print for beak appliqués

Clover bias tape maker (6 mm)

Basting glue

*Alma used a print with white dots for the owls' eyes. If your print doesn't have dots but you like the look of a highlight in the pupils, stitch a French knot with white embroidery floss in each eye.

Cutting

All measurements include ¼"-wide seam allowances.

From the black prints, cut a *total* of:
3 squares, 9½" × 9½"

From the black, cheddar, purple, and brown prints, cut a *total* of:
12 squares, 4½" × 4½"

HERE'S THE SKINNY ON
ALMA ALLEN & BARB ADAMS

The Blackbird Designs duo is always looking for ways to help us feather our nests with their strikingly beautiful designs. Their row is no exception; what a beauty (Blackbird-Designs.blogspot.com)!

Alma is currently obsessed with piecing baby quilts. "I love experimenting with new color combinations and patterns and really enjoy quilting them on my machine. It's just fun to see how they turn out, and then great giving them away too!"

She'd line up every time to get some salted caramel gelato. (The best!)

Our go-to sewing thread color is natural. We use it for 99% of our piecing.

The most productive time of day for Alma to sew is 8:00 to 10:00 a.m.

Alma's favorite marking tool is a chalk wheel. "I use it for quilting lines."

The last great series Alma binge-watched was *Stranger Things*.

Our go-to rotary cutters are 45 mm.

"My go-to scissors are anything I can find!" Alma says. "I have a hard time keeping track of them."

When pulling fabric for a single row like this, begin by choosing one color and then add to it.

Make the Appliqué Blocks

For illustrated information on appliqué, bias stems, and embroidery techniques, go to ShopMartingale.com/HowtoQuilt.

1 Using the bias tape maker, make three ¼" × 14" lengths of bias tape from the green print for the stems. Also make six ¼" × 1¾" lengths of bias tape from the brown solid for feet.

2 Using the patterns, opposite, prepare the shapes for turned-edge appliqué. Referring to the photo on page 39 as a guide, arrange and appliqué shapes onto the black print squares. Use basting glue to hold bias stems in place. For each foot, cut ½" through the center of each ¼" × 1¾" bias strip; spread the two edges of the strip apart about ¼" to form the claws. Turn under the raw edges, tapering the folded-under edge to nothing at the top of the ½" clip. Press the completed block and trim to 8½" square.

Appliqué placement

3 Appliqué a star on each of the print 4½" squares.

Assemble the Row

Referring to the photo on page 39, lay out the appliquéd Owl blocks and star units. Join the Star blocks into sections. Press the seam allowances in each section in opposite directions. Join the star sections and Owl blocks. The completed row should measure 8½" × 48½", including seam allowances.

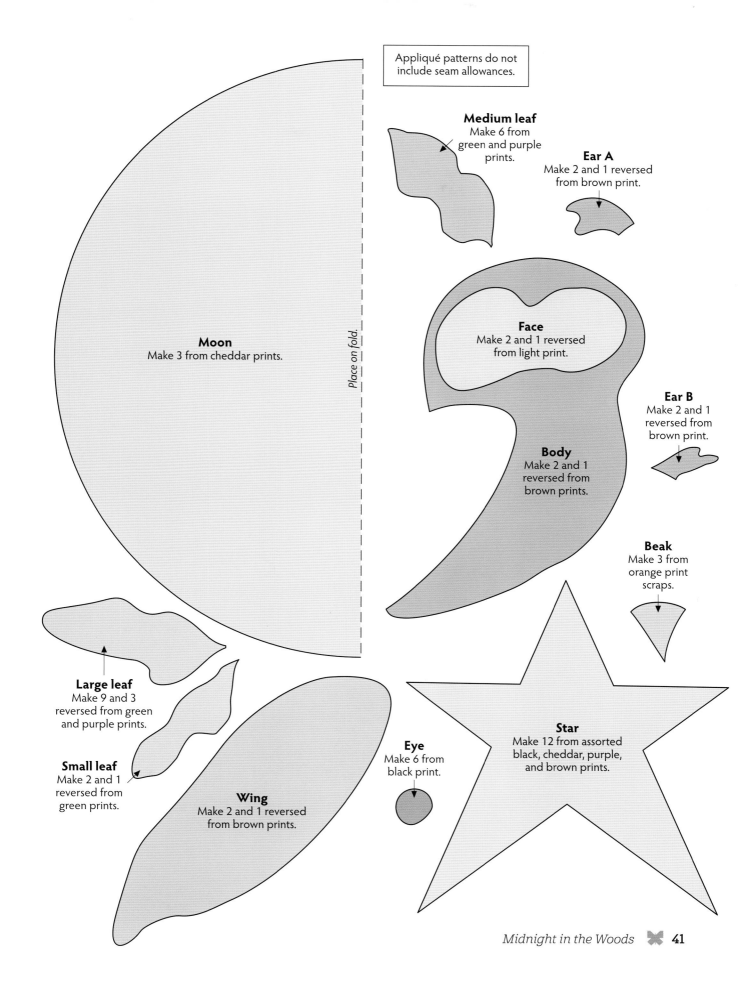

Appliqué patterns do not include seam allowances.

Medium leaf
Make 6 from green and purple prints.

Ear A
Make 2 and 1 reversed from brown print.

Moon
Make 3 from cheddar prints.

Place on fold

Face
Make 2 and 1 reversed from light print.

Ear B
Make 2 and 1 reversed from brown print.

Body
Make 2 and 1 reversed from brown prints.

Beak
Make 3 from orange print scraps.

Large leaf
Make 9 and 3 reversed from green and purple prints.

Small leaf
Make 2 and 1 reversed from green prints.

Wing
Make 2 and 1 reversed from brown prints.

Eye
Make 6 from black print.

Star
Make 12 from assorted black, cheddar, purple, and brown prints.

What a Hoot!

Designed by DEB STRAIN

FINISHED ROW: 10" × 48"

These wise old gentlemen, in their distinguished plaids and prints, are easy to appliqué using fusible web and machine stitching.

Materials

Yardage is based on 42"-wide fabric.

1½ yards of cream solid for background

10" × 10" square *each of 3* assorted yellow and blue prints for owl appliqués

5" × 5" square *each of 13* assorted brown, rust, yellow, blue, and black prints for owl appliqués

⅛ yard of brown print for stem appliqués

8" × 8" square *each of 2* green prints for leaf appliqués

7" × 7" square of black solid for outer eye, pupil, feet, and laughing-eye line appliqués

5" × 5" square of yellow print for feet and beak appliqués

5" × 5" square of white solid for inner eye appliqués

1¼ yards of 17"-wide lightweight paper-backed fusible web

Cutting

All measurements include ¼"-wide seam allowances.

From the *lengthwise grain* of the cream solid, cut:
1 strip, 10½" × 48½"

Appliqué the Row

For illustrated information on fusible appliqué, go to ShopMartingale.com/HowtoQuilt.

1 Using the patterns on pages 44 and 45, prepare the shapes for fusible appliqué.

2 Referring to the photo on page 42, arrange prepared shapes on background strip. Trim stems as necessary. Follow the manufacturer's instructions to fuse the shapes in place. Stitch around each appliqué using a zigzag stitch, blanket stitch, or stitch of your choice to permanently attach the shapes to the background. Or, stitch around each shape as part of the quilting, as Deb did. The completed row should measure 10½" × 48½", including seam allowances.

HERE'S THE SKINNY ON
DEB STRAIN

Her Saltbox Studio artwork might be more familiar to some on paper goods than fabric, but this talented artist has quilters loving her look on the bolt! (Find Deb Strain Studio on Facebook.)

I'm currently obsessed with collecting blue-and-white quilts.

I'd line up every time for a good restaurant.

The most productive time of day for me to sew is 7:00 to 9:00 a.m.

The last great series I binge-watched was *Game of Thrones*.

When designing my fabric collections, I usually begin with the panel art. A collection is like telling a story, for me, and the panel is the main idea.

If I'm stuck in a creative rut, I start looking through books or magazines or perusing Pinterest for inspiration. Thankfully, I usually have more ideas than I'll ever be able to develop!

One little tip that will make creating my row better is to look for contrast in the prints you choose for each owl. Easily seeing the distinction between pieces helps the owls pop!

Large owl body
Make 3 from asorted prints.

Leaf
Make 11 from
green prints.

Small owl head
Make 2 from
assorted prints.

Small owl body
Make 2 from
assorted prints.

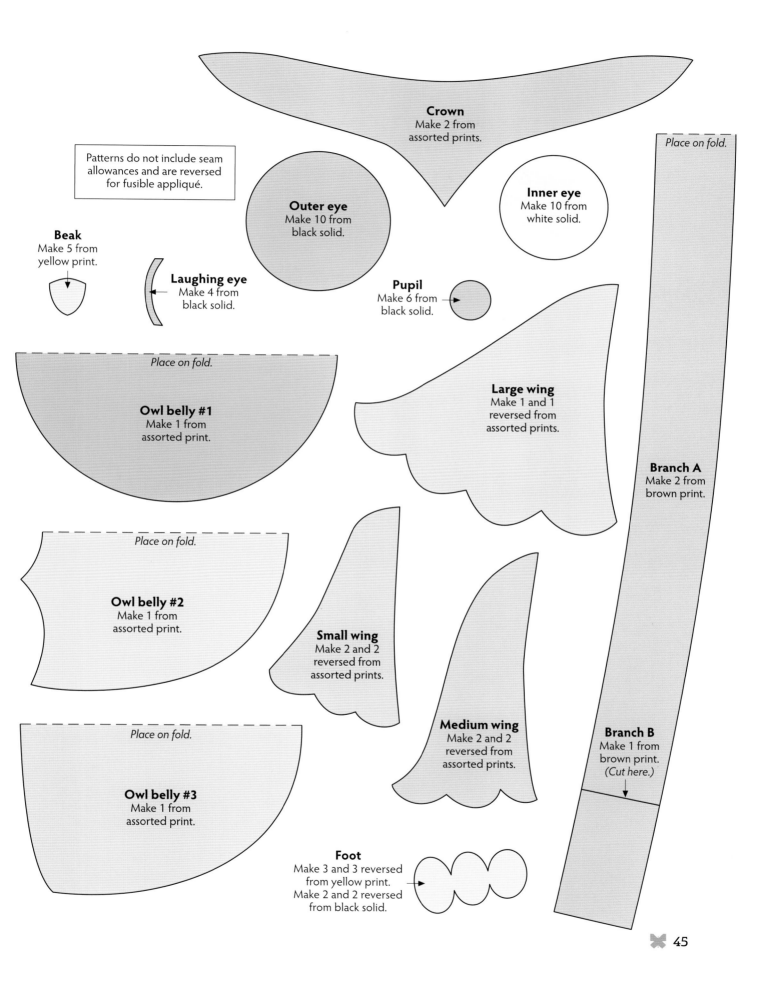

Crown
Make 2 from assorted prints.

Patterns do not include seam allowances and are reversed for fusible appliqué.

Outer eye
Make 10 from black solid.

Inner eye
Make 10 from white solid.

Place on fold.

Beak
Make 5 from yellow print.

Laughing eye
Make 4 from black solid.

Pupil
Make 6 from black solid.

Branch A
Make 2 from brown print.

Place on fold.

Owl belly #1
Make 1 from assorted print.

Large wing
Make 1 and 1 reversed from assorted prints.

Place on fold.

Owl belly #2
Make 1 from assorted print.

Small wing
Make 2 and 2 reversed from assorted prints.

Medium wing
Make 2 and 2 reversed from assorted prints.

Branch B
Make 1 from brown print.
(Cut here.)

Place on fold.

Owl belly #3
Make 1 from assorted print.

Foot
Make 3 and 3 reversed from yellow print.
Make 2 and 2 reversed from black solid.

45

Autumn Wind

Designed by **KATHY SCHMITZ** of Kathy Schmitz Studio

FINISHED ROW: 8" × 48"

Traditional piecing and hand embroidery are combined to make an autumnal row that's filled with texture.

Materials

Yardage is based on 42"-wide fabric. Fat quarters are 18"×21".

⅓ yard of light tan mottled print for embroidery background

⅓ yard of black print for pinwheels, pieced units, and embroidery blocks

1 fat quarter of medium tan print for pinwheels

1 fat quarter of tan-and-black print for pieced units

Water-soluble fabric marker or black fine-point permanent marker

Black 12-weight thread for embroidery

Size 7 hand-embroidery needle

Cutting

All measurements include ¼"-wide seam allowances.

From the light tan mottled print, cut:
2 rectangles, 10" × 12"

From the black print, cut:
28 squares, 3" × 3"
8 squares, 2½" × 2½"

From the medium tan print, cut:
14 squares, 3" × 3"

From the tan-and-black print, cut:
14 squares, 3" × 3"

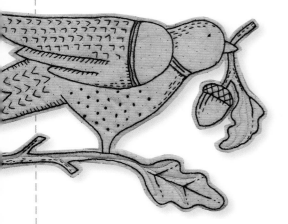

Make the Embroidery Blocks

Press all seam allowances as indicated by the arrows, or as otherwise instructed.

1 Trace the embroidery design on page 49 onto the right side of a light tan 10" × 12" rectangle using the fabric marker or black permanent pen. Trace the design again onto the wrong side of the remaining light tan 10" × 12" rectangle so it faces in the opposite direction on the right side. Retrace from the right side of the fabric.

2 Using one strand of the embroidery thread, stitch the design, working the solid lines with a stem stitch, the feathers with a fly stitch, the dots with French knots, and the dashed lines with a running stitch. For information on embroidery stitches, go to ShopMartingale.com/HowtoQuilt.

3 Press the embroidered blocks from the wrong side. Square up the stitched pieces to 8½" × 10½", keeping the design centered.

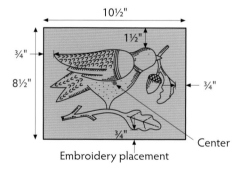

Embroidery placement

4 Draw a diagonal line from corner to corner on the wrong side of eight black 2½" squares. Layer a marked square on each corner of the embroidery blocks, right sides together as shown. Sew on the marked lines. Trim ¼" from the stitching lines. Press.

HERE'S THE SKINNY ON
KATHY SCHMITZ

Draw upon the experience of one of the quickest needles in the west—embroiderer and artist extraordinaire Kathy Schmitz. Mother Nature is her muse and we're all happy to share in the results of her gifted labor (KathySchmitz.com).

I'm currently obsessed with getting organized!

I'd line up every time to go to the Oregon coast.

My go-to sewing thread color is black. I use it for 80% of my embroidery.

The most productive time of day for me to embroider is 1:00 to 5:00 p.m.

My favorite marking tool is a Pilot Frixion pen. I use it for tracing my embroidery designs.

The last great series I binge-watched was *Sneaky Pete* (so good!).

My go-to rotary cutter is a 45 mm.

My go-to scissors are Kai embroidery scissors.

When pulling fabric for a single row like this, I begin by deciding on a background fabric for the embroidery.

One little tip that will make creating my row better is to enjoy the journey!

Make the Patchwork Units

1 Draw a diagonal line from corner to corner on the wrong side of each medium tan 3" square and each tan-and-black 3" square.

2 Layer a marked tan square on a black square, right sides together. Stitch ¼" from both sides of the marked line. Cut the squares on the line to make two half-square-triangle units. Repeat with the remaining marked squares and black squares to make a total of 28 half-square-triangle units. Trim each unit to 2½" square.

Make 28 units.

3 Lay out four half-square-triangle units in two rows of two as shown. Sew the units together in each row. Join the rows to make a Pinwheel block. Repeat to make a total of seven Pinwheel blocks.

Make 7 units,
4½" × 4½".

4 Using marked tan-and-black squares and remaining black print squares, repeat step 2 to make 28 half-square-triangle units.

5 Sew together 10 half-square-triangle units in a row. Press the seam allowances in one direction. Repeat to make a second pieced row.

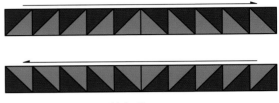

Make 2 rows,
2½" × 20½".

6 Sew together two half-square-triangle units to make a pair. Repeat to make two pairs. Make two pairs facing the opposite direction. Press the seam allowances open.

Make 2 units,
2½" × 4½".

Make 2 units,
2½" × 4½".

Assemble the Row

Lay out the embroidery blocks, Pinwheel blocks, pieced rows, and half-square-triangle pairs as shown below. Join the pieces into a row. The completed row should measure 8½" × 48½", including seam allowances.

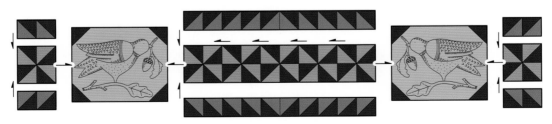

Row assembly

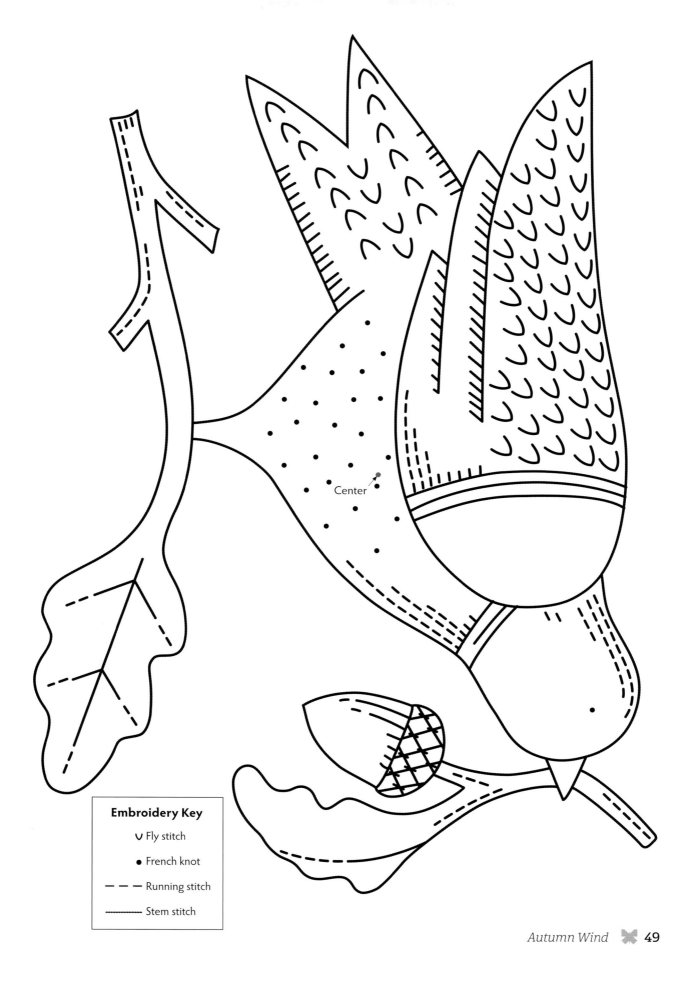

Center

Embroidery Key

∨ Fly stitch

● French knot

– – – Running stitch

········· Stem stitch

ROW QUILT GALLERY

How many rows could a quilter make if a quilter loves to make rows? No one knows for sure, but there's a good chance you'll find a long list of favorites as you peruse the collection of rows in this book again and again. To help get your creative juices flowing—whether you prefer to join your rows together in a larger quilt or finish and bind them one at a time—we've got a gallery of display ideas to spark your interest. Picture any of your favorite rows sprucing up your home decor. Then perhaps you'll be able to answer that first question!

Want more inspiration? Follow the "AllinaRowQuiltAlong" page on Facebook. Tag your rows and projects from the book with #allinarowquiltalong.

RIGHT: Not all rows have to read as horizontals. Here, Stars and Geese (page 86) is hung vertically from the back of a small wire shelf, ultimately spilling off the front for a dimensional display. A couple of coordinating moon and star accessories tie the whole look together.

OPPOSITE TOP: Invite your guests to take a closer look at your handwork. Create a coffee-table vignette with Pollen (page 10) that's sure to have them saying "can you make another for me?"

OPPOSITE BOTTOM: Play off the colors in a few of your favorite things. Love Fiestaware and its bold colors? Choose bright Bella solids that match your decor to build Barn Cute (page 68) for your home.

We give this charming row quilt a perfect ten! Combine five rows with five blender rows, toss in a scrappy assortment of warm-tone prints, and it all adds up to an inviting quilt. (Pieced by Tamra Dumolt; quilted by Karen Burns.)

For a row quilt that's guaranteed to look great, simplify the color palette. Blue and white set the stage for this two-color throw, keeping the emphasis on changes in hue. (Pieced by Susan Ache; quilted by Maggi Honeyman.)

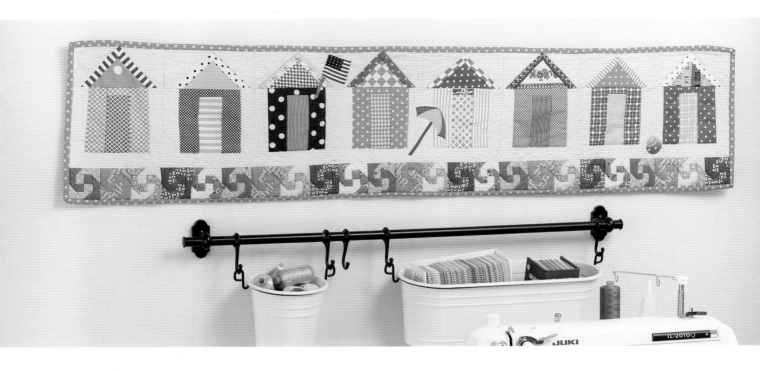

TOP: Take a vacation every time you sit down to sew. Hang Beach Houses (page 56) above your sewing table and each escape to your sewing room will be even more relaxing!

RIGHT: Don't limit your style to folded quilts on chair backs. Give Tricolor Stars (page 90) the starring role it deserves, draping it over a wooden rocker or favorite chair.

OPPOSITE TOP: Line the back of a beadboard shelf or cupboard with Autumn Wind (page 46), then nestle your stitchery and avian treasures together to create an eye-catching vignette.

OPPOSITE BOTTOM: Quilters are often collectors. Why not pair a collection of items, such as these artful flower frogs, with a like-themed Garden Time runner (page 25)?

Beach Houses

Designed by SANDY KLOP of American Jane Patterns

FINISHED ROW: 10" × 48"

Gather some fun prints for these beach houses. Before you know it, you'll be dreaming of glorious sunny days at the shore with the sound of the ocean lapping onto the sand.

Materials

Yardage is based on 42"-wide fabric. Fat quarters are 18" × 21".

½ yard *total* of assorted medium and dark prints for houses
¼ yard of beige solid for sand
1 fat quarter of light blue print for sky
6" × 12" rectangle *each of 10* assorted blue prints for Snail's Trail blocks
Scraps of 2 brown solids for poles of flag and umbrella
Scrap of red solid for umbrella
Scrap of yellow solid for umbrella
Printed flag for appliqué
Printed beach ball for appliqué
Template plastic
⅛ yard of 17"-wide lightweight paper-backed fusible web

Cutting

All measurements include ¼"-wide seam allowances. Trace patterns A–C on page 53 onto template plastic and cut them out. Use the templates to cut the block pieces from the fabrics indicated below.

From *each of 8* medium and dark prints, cut:
2 rectangles, 1¾" × 4¾" (16 total)
1 rectangle, 1" × 2" (8 total)

From the remaining medium and dark prints, cut a *total* of:
8 rectangles, 2" × 4¼", for doors
8 A pieces
8 B and 8 B reversed pieces (8 matching pairs of 1 B and 1 B reversed)

From the beige solid, cut:

4 strips, 1½" × 42"; crosscut *2 of the strips* into
16 rectangles, 1½" × 4¾"

From the light blue print, cut:

8 C and 8 C reversed pieces

From *each of the 10* blue prints, cut:

1 strip, 1" × 11" (10 total)

3 squares, 2¼" × 2¼" (30 total); cut the squares
into quarters diagonally to yield 12 small
triangles (120 total; from each print, you'll use
10 and have 2 left over)

5 squares, 1⅞" × 1⅞" (50 total); cut the squares
in half diagonally to yield 10 large triangles
(100 total)

Make the House Blocks

Press all seam allowances as indicated by the
arrows, or as otherwise instructed.

1 Lay out two matching 1¾" × 4¾" print rectangles
and one 1" × 2" rectangle; one 2" × 4¼" door
rectangle; and two beige 1½" × 4¾" rectangles as
shown. Sew the rectangles together to make a house
unit. The house unit should measure 4¾" × 6½".
Repeat to make a total of eight house units.

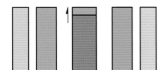 

Make 8 units,
4¾" × 6½".

2 Sew a B piece to the left edge of an A roof
piece; stop stitching at the top seamline and
backstitch. Add the matching B reversed piece to
the right edge of the A roof piece in the same
manner. Stitch the short edges of the B and B
reversed pieces together as shown to miter the top
of the roof. Add a light blue C piece and a light blue

C reversed piece to complete a roof unit. The roof
unit should measure 6½" × 3¼". Repeat to make a
total of eight roof units.

Make 8 units,
3¼" × 6½".

3 Sew a roof unit to the top of a house unit
to make a House block. The block should
measure 6½" × 7½". Repeat to make a total of
eight House blocks.

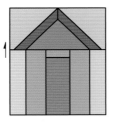

Make 8 House blocks,
6½" × 7½".

Make the Snail's Trail Blocks

To make a set of five matching blocks, gather pieces
cut from two blue prints. Repeat the assembly steps
to make five sets of five matching blocks.

1 Sew two contrasting blue 1" × 11" strips together
to make a strip set as shown. From the strip set,
cut 10 segments, 1" wide.

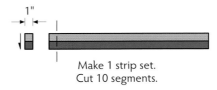

1"

Make 1 strip set.
Cut 10 segments.

2 Sew the segments together in pairs to make five center units, 1½" square.

Make 5 units,
1½" × 1½".

3 Sew a pair of matching small triangles to opposite edges of each center unit. Sew a second pair of matching small triangles to each unit. The units should be 2" square.

4 Sew a pair of matching large triangles to a unit as shown. Sew a second pair of matching large triangles to the unit to complete a block. The block should measure 2½" square. Repeat to make a total of five matching Snail's Trail blocks.

Make 5 matching blocks,
(25 total, 1 is extra)
2½" × 2½".

Assemble the Row

1 Lay out the House blocks side by side in a horizontal row. Join the blocks and press the seam allowances in one direction.

2 Join the two remaining beige 1½" × 42" strips end to end. Trim the strip to 48½" long and sew it to the bottom of the House row. Press the seam allowances toward the beige strip.

3 Sew together the 24 Snail's Trail blocks side by side. Press the seam allowances in one direction. Join this row to the bottom of the beige strip and press the seam allowances toward the beige strip. The completed row should measure 10½" × 48½", including seam allowances.

Appliqué the Row

For more information on fusible appliqué, go to ShopMartingale.com/HowtoQuilt.

1 Using the patterns below, prepare the shapes for fusible appliqué.

2 Referring to the photo on page 50 as a guide, appliqué the flagpole and flag to one house. Appliqué the umbrella pole and umbrella pieces between two houses. Appliqué the beach ball on the sand.

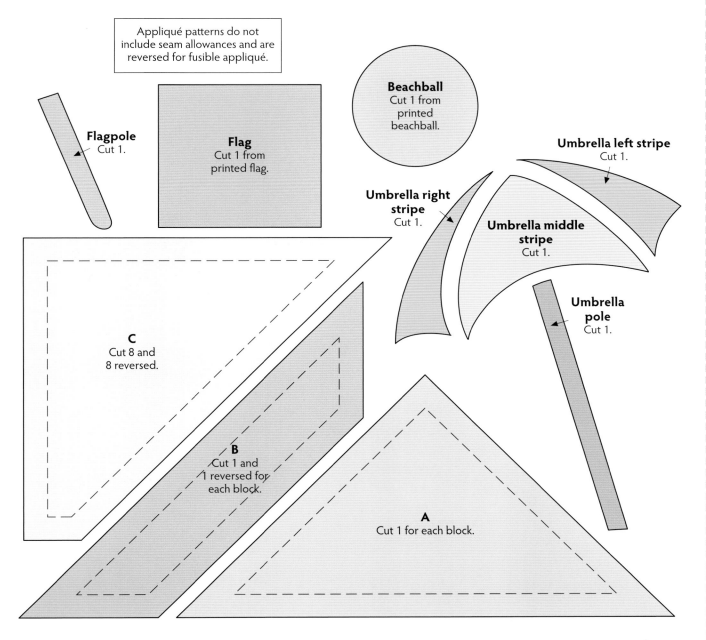

Appliqué patterns do not include seam allowances and are reversed for fusible appliqué.

Flagpole
Cut 1.

Flag
Cut 1 from printed flag.

Beachball
Cut 1 from printed beachball.

Umbrella left stripe
Cut 1.

Umbrella right stripe
Cut 1.

Umbrella middle stripe
Cut 1.

Umbrella pole
Cut 1.

C
Cut 8 and 8 reversed.

B
Cut 1 and 1 reversed for each block.

A
Cut 1 for each block.

Picket Fences

Designed by SANDY GERVAIS

FINISHED ROW: 10" × 48"

Stitch a street of quaint little houses bordered by picket fences. And just so everyone knows quilters live there, two houses have pinwheel blocks on the front!

Materials

Yardage is based on 42"-wide fabric. Fat eighths are 9" × 21".

¾ yard of blue solid for background
5" × 5" square *each of 4 assorted brown prints for roofs*
1" × 2½" rectangle *each of 3 assorted solids for chimneys*
1 fat eighth *each of 8 assorted prints for houses*
1 fat eighth of white solid for windows, pinwheels, doors, and fences
5" × 8" rectangle of tan solid for fences
⅛ yard of 17"-wide lightweight paper-backed fusible web

Cutting

All measurements include ¼"-wide seam allowances.

From the *lengthwise* grain of the blue solid, cut:
4 strips, 1" × 26"

From the *crosswise* grain of the blue solid, cut a *total* of:
2 rectangles, 7" × 8½"
2 rectangles, 3½" × 4½"
3 rectangles, 2½" × 4½"
13 squares, 2½" × 2½"
3 rectangles, 1½" × 2½"
4 rectangles, 1⅝" × 2"
3 rectangles, 1" × 2½"
8 rectangles, 1" × 2"
8 rectangles, 1" × 1⅜"

From the assorted brown prints, cut a *total* of:

8 rectangles, 2½" × 4½"

From *each of 2* assorted prints, cut:

2 rectangles, 1½" × 4½" (4 total)

2 rectangles, 1½" × 2½" (4 total)

2 squares, 1⅞" × 1⅞"; cut the squares in half
diagonally to yield 4 triangles (8 total)

From *each of 3* assorted prints, cut:

1 rectangle, 4½" × 7½" (3 total)

From *each of 3* assorted prints, cut:

1 rectangle, 4½" × 5½" (3 total)

From the white solid, cut:

4 squares, 1⅞" × 1⅞"; cut the squares in half
diagonally to yield 8 triangles

10 rectangles, 1¼" × 2"

From the tan solid, cut:

4 strips, 1" × 6¾"

Make the Roof Units

Press all seam allowances as indicated by the
arrows, or as otherwise instructed.

1 Draw a diagonal line on the wrong side of each
blue 2½" square. Layer a marked square on a
brown rectangle, right sides together. Stitch on the
line as shown. Trim ¼" from the stitching line and
press. Repeat on the opposite end of the rectangle
to make a roof unit. Repeat to make a total of five
roof units.

Make 5 units,
2½" × 4½".

2 Sew a blue 1½" × 2½" rectangle to the left side
of a solid 1" × 2½" chimney rectangle and a blue
1" × 2½" rectangle to the right side as shown.
Repeat to make a total of three chimney squares.

Make 3 units,
2½" × 2½".

3 Draw a diagonal line from corner to corner on
the wrong side of each chimney square as
shown. Be sure that the chimney rectangle is
horizontal, and the narrow blue rectangle is on the
bottom. Layer one chimney square on a brown
rectangle as shown. Stitch on the line. Trim ¼" from
the stitching line. Repeat on the opposite end of the
rectangle using a blue 2½" square. The chimney unit
should be 2½" × 4½". Repeat to make a total of
three chimney units.

Make 3 units,
2½" × 4½".

4 Sew a blue 2½" × 4½" rectangle to each of two
roof units from step 1 as shown. Sew a blue
2½" × 4½" rectangle to one chimney unit. Sew a
blue 3½" × 4½" rectangle to each of two roof units.

Make 2 units,
4½" × 4½".

Make 1 unit,
4½" × 4½".

Make 2 units,
4½" × 5½".

Make the House Section

1 Sew a print triangle to a white triangle to make a half-square-triangle unit. Press, and trim the dog ears. The unit should measure 1½" square. Repeat to make a total of eight half-square-triangle units (two sets of four matching units).

Make 8 units
(2 sets of 4 matching),
1½" × 1½".

2 Lay out four matching half-square-triangle units as shown. Sew the units together in each row. Join the rows to make a pinwheel unit. The pinwheel unit should measure 2½" square. Repeat to make a total of two pinwheel units.

Make 2 units,
2½" × 2½".

3 Sew matching print 1½" × 2½" rectangles to opposite sides of a pinwheel unit as shown. Sew the matching print 1½" × 4½" rectangles to the top and bottom of the unit. The pinwheel house unit should measure 4½" square. Repeat to make a second pinwheel house unit.

Make 2 units,
4½" × 4½".

4 Referring to the photo on page 54, sew one roof unit or chimney unit to each 4½" × 7½" and 4½" × 5½" house rectangle and each pinwheel house unit to make eight House blocks. Press the seam allowances toward the roof or chimney unit. Each block should measure 4½" × 9½".

5 Prepare two white windows, 1" × 1½"; five tall white doors, 1" × 2¾"; and one short white door, 1" × 1¾", for fusible appliqué. For illustrated information on fusible appliqué, go to ShopMartingale.com/HowtoQuilt. Referring to the photo as needed, position the windows and doors on the House blocks. Follow the manufacturer's instructions to fuse the pieces in place. Stitch around each appliqué using a zigzag stitch, blanket stitch, or stitch of your choice to permanently attach the shapes to the background.

6 Join the House blocks side by side in a row. Press the seam allowances toward the taller houses. The house section should measure 9½" × 32½".

Make the Fence Sections

1 Join five white 1¼" × 2" rectangles and four blue 1" × 2" rectangles, alternating them as shown. Sew a blue 1⅝" × 2" rectangle to each end to make a picket unit. Repeat to make a total of two picket units. Each unit should measure 2" × 8½".

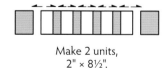

Make 2 units,
2" × 8½".

2 Sew a blue 1" × 1⅜" rectangle to each end of a tan strip as shown to make a railing unit. Repeat to make a total of four railing units that are 1" × 8½".

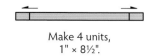

Make 4 units,
1" × 8½".

3 Lay out one picket unit, two railing units, and one blue 7" × 8½" rectangle as shown. Join the pieces. The fence section should measure 8½" × 9½". Repeat to make a total of two fence sections.

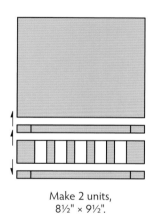

Make 2 units,
8½" × 9½".

Assemble the Row

1 Join the house section and fence sections. Press the seam allowances toward the house section.

2 Join two blue 1" × 26" strips end to end. Press the seam allowances open. Repeat to make two pieced strips. Trim the pieced strips to 48½" long. Sew the strips to the top and bottom of the row. Press the seam allowances toward the strips. The completed row should measure 10½" × 48½", including seam allowances.

Treetop Neighborhood

Designed by BRENDA RIDDLE of Acorn Quilt & Gift Company

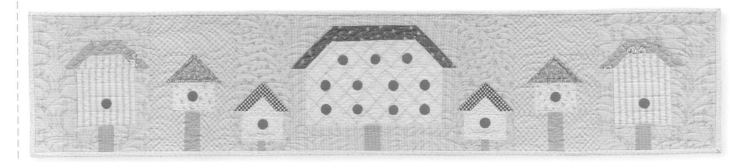

FINISHED ROW: 10" × 48"

Birdhouses are not just for birds. These cute houses, side by side, make an adorable addition to a row quilt.

Materials

Yardage is based on 42"-wide fabric. Fat quarters are 18" × 21". Fat eighths are 9" × 21".

2 fat quarters and 2 fat eighths of assorted blue prints for background

1 fat eighth *each of 4* assorted light prints for birdhouses

10" × 10" square *each of 4* assorted prints for roofs

10" × 10" square of gray solid for poles

5" × 5" square of brown for hole appliqués

⅛ yard of 17"-wide lightweight paper-backed fusible web

Cutting

All measurements include ¼"-wide seam allowances. This quilt features 4 different styles of birdhouses, designated A–D. You'll need to make 2 each of A, B, and C, and 1 of D.

BIRDHOUSE A

Cutting is for 2 blocks.

From 1 blue print fat quarter, cut:

2 squares, 3" × 3"; cut the squares in half diagonally to yield 4 triangles

2 rectangles, 2½" × 10½"

2 rectangles, 2½" × 6½"

4 rectangles, 2" × 2½"

4 rectangles, 1½" × 6½"

From 1 light print, cut:

2 squares, 4½" × 4½"

2 rectangles, 1½" × 2½"

4 squares, 1½" × 1½"

From 1 roof print, cut:

2 squares, 3" × 3"; cut the squares in half diagonally to yield 4 triangles

2 rectangles, 1½" × 2½"

From the gray solid, cut:

2 rectangles, 1½" × 2½"

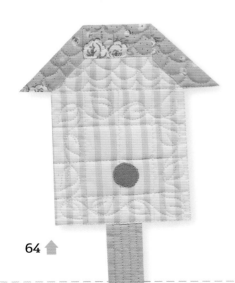

BIRDHOUSE B

Cutting is for 2 blocks.

From 1 blue print fat quarter, cut:
2 rectangles, 3½" × 6½"
4 rectangles, 3" × 3½"
4 squares, 2½" × 2½"
4 rectangles, 2" × 2½"
4 rectangles, 1½" × 2½"

From 1 light print, cut:
2 rectangles, 2½" × 3½"

From 1 roof print, cut:
2 rectangles, 2½" × 4½"

From the gray solid, cut:
2 rectangles, 1½" × 3½"

BIRDHOUSE C

Cutting is for 2 blocks.

From 1 blue print fat eighth, cut:
2 rectangles, 4½" × 5½"
2 squares, 3" × 3"; cut the
    squares in half diagonally
    to yield 4 triangles
4 rectangles, 1½" × 2¼"
4 rectangles, 1" × 2½"

From 1 light print, cut:
2 rectangles, 2½" × 3½"
4 squares, 1½" × 1½"

From 1 roof print, cut:
2 squares, 3" × 3"; cut the
    squares in half diagonally
    to yield 4 triangles

From the gray solid, cut:
2 rectangles, 1" × 1½"

BIRDHOUSE D

Cutting is for 1 block.

From 1 blue print fat eighth, cut:
2 squares, 4" × 4"; cut the
    squares in half diagonally
    (but in opposite directions)
    to yield 2 triangles with stripe
    going in opposite directions.
2 rectangles, 2½" × 6"
1 strip, 1½" × 12½"
2 rectangles, 1½" × 4½"

From 1 light print, cut:
1 rectangle, 4½" × 10½"
1 rectangle, 2½" × 6½"
2 squares, 2½" × 2½"

From 1 roof print, cut:
1 square, 4" × 4"; cut the square
    in half diagonally to yield 2
    triangles
1 rectangle, 1½" × 6½"

From the gray solid, cut:
1 rectangle, 1½" × 2½"

Make Birdhouse A

Press all seam allowances as indicated by the arrows, or as otherwise instructed.

1 Sew a blue triangle and a roof print triangle together to make a half-square-triangle unit. Repeat to make a total of four half-square-triangle units. Trim each unit to 2½" square.

2½"

2½"

Make 4 units.

2 Draw a diagonal line from corner to corner on the wrong side of each light 1½" square. Layer a marked square on a half-square-triangle unit, right sides together as shown. Stitch on the line. Trim ¼" from the stitching line to make a side roof unit. Repeat to make a total of four side roof units.

Make 4 units,
2½" × 2½".

3 Lay out one roof print 1½" × 2½" rectangle, one light 1½" × 2½" rectangle, two side roof units, and one blue 2½" × 6½" rectangle as shown. Join the pieces to make a roof section. Repeat to make a total of two roof sections that measure 4½" × 6½".

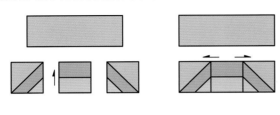

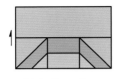

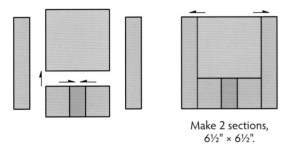

Make 2 sections,
4½" × 6½".

4 Lay out one light 4½" square, two blue 2" × 2½" rectangles, one gray solid rectangle, and two blue 1½" × 6½" rectangles as shown. Join the pieces to make a house section. Repeat to make two house sections that are 6½" square.

Make 2 sections,
6½" × 6½".

5 Join a roof section and a house section; press. Add a blue 2½" × 10½" strip to the left edge of the joined sections to make the left Birdhouse A block. Repeat, adding a blue strip to the right edge

to make the right Birdhouse A block. The blocks should measure 8½" × 10½".

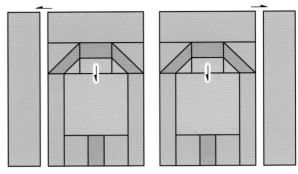

Birdhouse A.
Make one of each,
8½" × 10½".

Make Birdhouse B

1 Draw a diagonal line from corner to corner on the wrong side of each blue 2½" square. Layer a marked square on a 2½" × 4½" roof rectangle, right sides together. Sew on the marked line. Trim ¼" from stitching line and press. Repeat on the opposite end of the rectangle as shown to complete a roof unit. Make two.

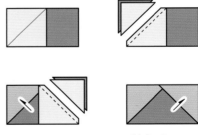

Make 2 units,
2½" × 4½".

2 Join a roof unit, two blue 1½" × 2½" rectangles, and one blue 3½" × 6½" rectangle as shown to make a roof section that is 5½" × 6½. Make two.

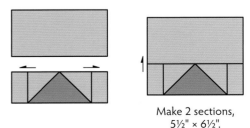

Make 2 sections,
5½" × 6½".

3 Lay out one light rectangle, two blue 2" × 2½" rectangles, two blue 3" × 3½" rectangles, and one gray solid rectangle as shown. Join the pieces to make a house section. Repeat to make two house sections that measure 5½" × 6½".

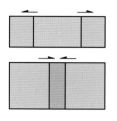 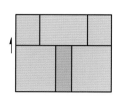

Make 2 sections,
5½" × 6½".

4 Join a roof section and a house section to make a Birdhouse B block. Repeat to make two total. The blocks should measure 6½" × 10½".

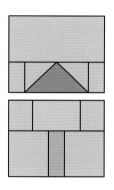 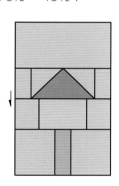

Birdhouse B.
Make 2 blocks,
6½" × 10½".

Make Birdhouse C

1 Sew a blue triangle and a roof triangle together to make a half-square-triangle unit. Repeat to make four units. Trim each unit to 2½" square.

Make 4 units.

2 Draw a diagonal line from corner to corner on the wrong side of each light 1½" square as shown. Layer one marked square on a half-square-triangle unit, right sides together. Stitch on the line.

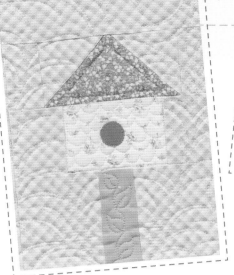 

Trim ¼" from the stitching line to make one roof unit. Repeat to make four roof units.

Make 4 units,
2½" × 2½".

3 Join two roof units and a blue 4½" × 5½" rectangle as shown to make a roof section. Repeat to make two roof sections that are 4½" × 7½".

  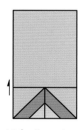

Make 2 sections,
4½" × 7½".

4 Lay out one light 2½" × 3½" rectangle, two blue 1" × 2½" rectangles, two blue 1½" × 2¼" rectangles, and one gray solid rectangle as shown. Join the pieces to make a house section. Repeat to make two house sections that measure 3½" × 4½".

Make 2 sections,
3½" × 4½".

5 Join a roof section and a house section to make a Birdhouse C block. Repeat to make two total. The blocks should measure 4½" × 10½".

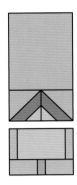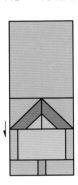

Birdhouse C.
Make 2 blocks,
4½" × 10½".

Make Birdhouse D

1 Sew one blue triangle and one roof triangle together to make a half-square-triangle unit. Repeat to make a second unit angled in the opposite direction. Trim both units to 3½" square.

Make 1 of each unit.

2 Draw a diagonal line from corner to corner on the wrong side of each light 2½" square as shown. Layer one marked square on a half-square-triangle unit, right sides together. Stitch on the line. Trim ¼" from the stitching line to make a side roof unit. Repeat to make two.

Make 2 units, 3½" × 3½".

3 Lay out the side roof units, light 2½" × 6½" rectangle, 1½" × 6½" roof rectangle, and blue 1½" × 12½" strip as shown. If using a stripe, lay out all pieces with stripes going in the same direction. Join the pieces to make the roof section.

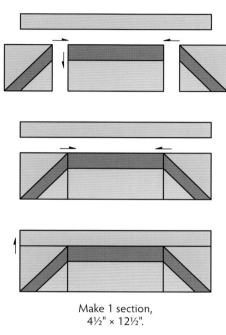

Make 1 section,
4½" × 12½".

4 Lay out the light 4½" × 10½" rectangle, blue 1½" × 4½" rectangles, blue 2½" × 6" rectangles, and gray solid rectangle as shown. Join the pieces to make the house section.

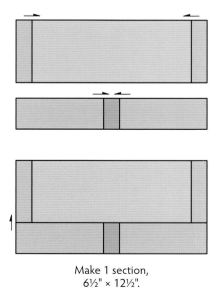

Make 1 section,
6½" × 12½".

5 Join the roof section and house section to make the Birdhouse D block. The block should measure 10½" × 12½".

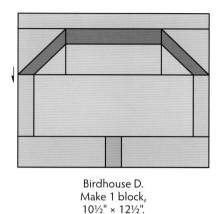

Birdhouse D.
Make 1 block,
10½" × 12½".

Appliqué the Holes

Using the pattern below and the brown 5" square, prepare 17 circles for fusible appliqué. For illustrated information on fusible appliqué, go to ShopMartingale.com/HowtoQuilt. Referring to the photo on page 58 as needed, position the circles on the Birdhouse blocks. Follow the manufacturer's instructions to fuse the pieces in place. Stitch around each appliqué using a zigzag or small buttonhole stitch.

Assemble the Row

Lay out the Birdhouse blocks side by side in a horizontal row. Join the blocks and press the seam allowances open. The completed row should measure 10½" × 48½", including seam allowances.

Circle
Make 17.

Pattern does not include
seam allowance.

Painted Ladies

Designed by **BARBARA GROVES AND MARY JACOBSON of Me and My Sister Designs**

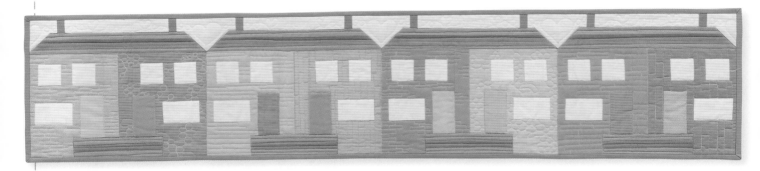

FINISHED ROW: 10" × 48"

Piece brightly colored town houses using either solids or prints, or both for variety, just like a real community.

Materials

Yardage is based on 42"-wide fabric.

¼ yard of light gray solid for steps and roofs

⅛ yard of medium gray solid for steps, chimneys, and roofs

¼ yard of white solid for windows and background

10" × 10" square *each of 8* assorted solids for houses and doors

Cutting

All measurements include ¼"-wide seam allowances.

From the light gray solid, cut:
4 strips, 1" × 42"

From the medium gray solid, cut:
3 strips, 1" × 42"; crosscut *1 of the strips* into 8 rectangles, 1" × 1½"

From the white solid, cut:
2 strips, 2" × 42"; crosscut into:
    8 rectangles, 2" × 3"
    24 squares, 2" × 2"
2 strips, 1½" × 42"; crosscut into:
    4 rectangles, 1½" × 7½"
    8 rectangles, 1½" × 2½"

From *each of the 8* assorted solids, cut:
2 rectangles, 2" × 3½" (16 total)
1 rectangle, 1½" × 6½" (8 total)
1 rectangle, 1½" × 4" (8 total)
2 rectangles, 1¼" × 5½" (16 total)
2 rectangles, 1¼" × 2" (16 total)
1 rectangle, 1" × 4" (8 total)
3 rectangles, 1" × 2" (24 total)

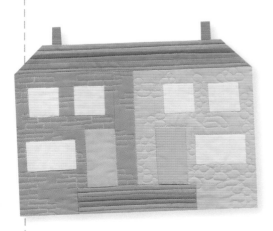

Make the Roof Units

Press all seam allowances as indicated by the arrows, or as otherwise instructed.

1 Sew two light gray strips and one medium gray strip together to make a strip set as shown. Repeat to make a total of two strip sets. From *each* strip set, cut two segments, 2" × 12½", and two segments, 2" × 6½".

Make 2 strip sets.
Cut 2 of each segment from each strip set
(4 total of each segment).

2 Draw a diagonal line from corner to corner on the wrong side of eight white 2" squares. Layer two marked squares on one 12½" strip-set segment, right sides together as shown. Sew on the marked lines. Trim the seam allowances to ¼". Press the seam allowances toward the corner to make a roof unit. Repeat to make a total of four roof units.

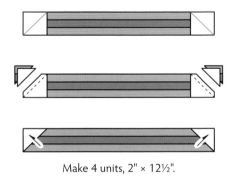

Make 4 units, 2" × 12½".

3 Lay out two white 1½" × 2½" rectangles, one white 1½" × 7½" rectangle, and two medium gray 1" × 1½" rectangles as shown. Sew the rectangles together. Repeat to make a total of four chimney units, 1½" × 12½".

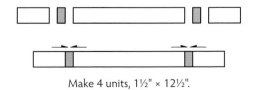

Make 4 units, 1½" × 12½".

4 Join a chimney unit and a roof unit. The roof should measure 3" × 12½". Repeat to make a total of four roof units.

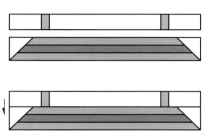

Make 4 units, 3" × 12½".

Make the Blocks

1 Lay out two white 2" squares and the following matching rectangles: two 1¼" × 5½", two 1¼" × 2", and one 1" × 2". Sew the pieces together as shown to make an upstairs unit, 3½" × 5½". Repeat to make a total of eight upstairs units.

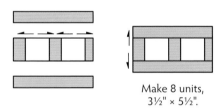

Make 8 units,
3½" × 5½".

2 Lay out one white 2" × 3" rectangle and the following matching rectangles: two 1" × 2", one 1" × 4", and one 1½" × 4". Sew the pieces together as shown. Add one contrasting 2" × 3½" rectangle to make a door unit, 3½" × 5½". Repeat to make a total of eight door units—four with the door on the right and four with the door on the left.

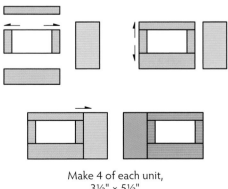

Make 4 of each unit,
3½" × 5½".

3 Lay out one upstairs unit, the matching door unit, and the matching 1½" × 6½" rectangle as shown. Sew the pieces together to make a left unit, and press the seam allowances as indicated. Make four left units. Repeat to make four right units with the door on the opposite side as shown.

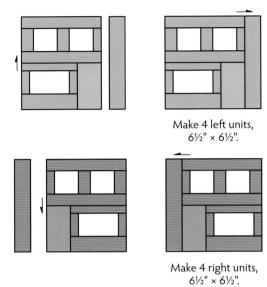

Make 4 left units,
6½" × 6½".

Make 4 right units,
6½" × 6½".

4 For one block, choose a left unit and a right unit. Gather one 2" × 3½" rectangle to match the left unit and one 2" × 3½" rectangle to match the right unit. Sew the rectangles to one 6½" strip-set segment to make a step unit as shown. Repeat to make four step units, each 2" × 12½".

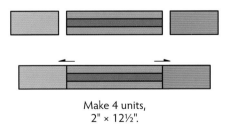

Make 4 units,
2" × 12½".

If solids aren't your thing, think about creating adorable printed houses.

5 Lay out a left unit, right unit, step unit, and roof unit as shown. Sew the units together to make one block, 12½" × 10½". Repeat to make a total of four blocks.

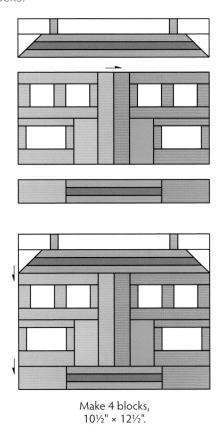

Make 4 blocks,
10½" × 12½".

Assemble the Row

Lay out the blocks side by side in a horizontal row. Join the blocks and press the seam allowances in one direction. The completed row should measure 10½" × 48½", including seam allowances.

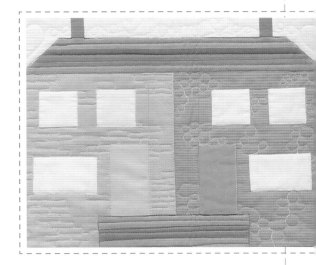

Barn Cute

Designed by **KATE SPAIN**

FINISHED ROW: 10" × 48"

Quilt blocks on barns are all the rage! Solid colors keep the effect simple and accentuate the design.

Materials

Yardage is based on 42"-wide fabric. Fat quarters are 18"×21". Fat eighths are 9"×21".

1 fat quarter of white solid for background
1 fat eighth *each of 4* solids (red, blue, aqua, and charcoal) for barns and roofs
10" × 10" square *each of 6* solids (light green, dark green, turquoise, bright pink, light pink, and navy) for barns
Template plastic

Cutting

All measurements include ¼"-wide seam allowances. Trace patterns A and B on page 74 onto template plastic and cut them out. Use the templates to cut the pieces from the fabrics indicated below.

From the white solid, cut:
4 strips, 1½" × 21"; crosscut into:
    4 strips, 1½" × 10½"
    2 strips, 1½" × 7½"
    12 squares, 1½" × 1½"
1 strip, 2½" × 21"; crosscut into:
    4 rectangles, 2½" × 3"
    2 squares, 2½" × 2½"
1 A and 1 A reversed piece

From the red solid, cut:
1 rectangle, 3½" × 8½"
1 strip, 2½" × 6½"
1 strip, 1½" × 5½"
1 strip, 1" × 7½"
8 squares, 1¾" × 1¾"

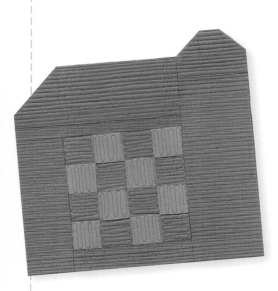

From the blue solid, cut:
2 rectangles, 3" × 7½"
2 rectangles, 2½" × 3½"
2 strips, 2" × 5½"
1 strip, 1½" × 8½"
1 strip, 1" × 8½"

From the aqua solid, cut:
2 strips, 2" × 5½"
1 strip, 1½" × 8½"
1 strip, 1" × 8½"
4 rectangles, 1¾" × 3"
4 squares, 1¾" × 1¾"

From the charcoal solid, cut:
2 strips, 2" × 8½"
2 rectangles, 2½" × 3½"
1 B piece

From the light green solid, cut:
1 rectangle, 3½" × 8½"
1 strip, 2½" × 6½"
1 strip, 1½" × 5½"
1 strip, 1" × 7½"

From the dark green solid, cut:
8 squares, 1¾" × 1¾"

From the turquoise solid, cut:
2 squares, 3½" × 3½"
8 squares, 1¾" × 1¾"

From the bright pink solid, cut:
2 squares, 3½" × 3½"
1 square, 3" × 3"
8 squares, 1¾" × 1¾"

From the light pink solid, cut:
1 strip, 1½" × 8½"
1 strip, 1" × 8½"
2 strips, 2" × 5½"

From the navy solid, cut:
4 squares, 3½" × 3½"
8 squares, 1¾" × 1¾"

Make the Checkerboard Barn Blocks

Press all seam allowances as indicated by the arrows, or as otherwise instructed.

1 Lay out eight dark green squares and eight turquoise 1¾" squares in four rows of four. Sew the squares together in each row. Join the rows to make a checkerboard unit. The unit should be 5½" square. Repeat to make a checkerboard unit using eight bright pink 1¾" squares and eight red squares.

2 Sew the red 1½" × 5½" strip to the bottom of the turquoise/green checkerboard unit as shown. Sew the red 2½" × 6½" strip to the left side and the red 1" × 7½" strip to the top to make a barn unit. The barn unit should be 7" × 7½". Repeat to make a barn unit with the pink/red checkerboard unit and light green strips.

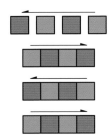

Make 1 of each colorway, 5½" × 5½".

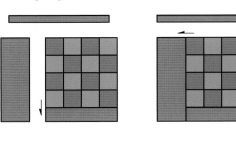
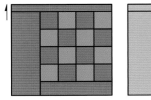
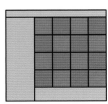

Make 1 of each colorway, 7" × 7½".

6 Join the red barn unit, red silo unit, one roof unit, and one white 1½" × 7½" strip as shown to make a Checkerboard Barn block. Repeat to make a light green Checkerboard Barn block.

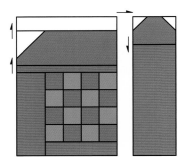

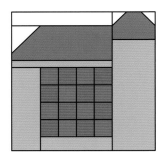

Make 1 Checkerboard Barn block
of each colorway, 10½" × 10½".

3 Draw a diagonal line from corner to corner on the wrong side of each white 2½" and 1½" square. Layer a marked 2½" square on the top left of a blue 3" × 7½" rectangle, right sides together. Stitch on the line as shown. Trim ¼" from the line and press. Repeat to make two roof units.

Make 2 units,
3" × 7½".

4 In the same manner, layer marked white 1½" squares on the top left and right corners of a blue 2½" × 3½" rectangle. Stitch, trim, and press as before. Make two.

Make 2 units,
2½" × 3½".

5 Sew one unit from step 4 to a red 3½" × 8½" rectangle to complete a silo unit. Repeat to make a silo unit using the light green 3½" × 8½" rectangle. Each silo should measure 3½" × 10½".

Make the Pinwheel Barn Blocks

1 Draw a diagonal line from corner to corner on the wrong side of each bright pink 3½" square. Layer a marked square on a navy 3½" square, right sides together. Stitch ¼" from the line on both sides. Cut on the line to yield two half-square-triangle units. Repeat to make four. Trim the units to 3" square. Using turquoise instead of pink, make four half-square-triangle units.

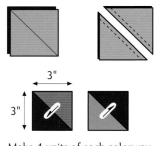

Make 4 units of each colorway,
3" × 3".

2 Lay out the half-square-triangle units in two rows of two as shown. Sew the units together in each row. Join the rows to make a pinwheel unit. The unit should be 5½" square. Repeat to make a turquoise/navy pinwheel unit.

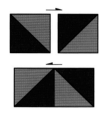

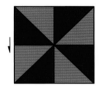

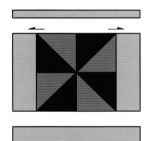

Make 1 unit of each colorway,
5½" × 5½".

3 Sew the aqua 2" × 5½" strips to the sides of the pink/navy pinwheel unit. Sew the aqua 1" × 8½" strip to the top of the unit and the aqua 1½" × 8½" strip to the bottom to make a barn unit. The barn unit should measure 7" × 8½". Repeat to make a light pink barn unit using the turquoise/navy pinwheel unit.

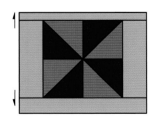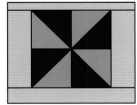

Make 1 unit of each colorway,
7" × 8½".

HERE'S THE SKINNY ON
KATE SPAIN

We wish we lived on or around the farm that Kate's row depicts. You're sure to reap what you sow (or is it sew?) with this artful array of pretty quilted barns (kdspain.com).

I'm currently obsessed with my new slow-cooker.

I'd line up every time for a plant sale at our local garden center.

The most productive time of day for me to create is between 7:30 and 9:30 a.m.

The last great series I binge-watched was *Breaking Bad* (and then we cancelled our cable).

When designing my fabric collections, I usually begin by drawing or painting to get some initial ideas on paper. While I work on the designs, I begin to envision a color palette and from there I get whisked off into the process.

If I'm stuck in a creative rut, I leave what I'm working on and switch materials. If I'm drawing, then I'll paint or carve woodblocks, or cut paper, or sew. Sometimes just changing the size of a paintbrush will make everything look different, which jump-starts the design process again.

One little tip that will make creating my row more fun is to alter the direction and style of your machine quilting to add different textures to the barn exteriors (think clapboard and shingles)!

6 Sew white 2½" × 3" rectangles to opposite sides of a unit from step 5 to make a cupola unit. The unit should measure 2½" × 8½". Repeat to make a total of two cupola units.

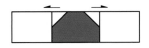

Make 2 units,
2½" × 8½".

7 Lay out the aqua barn unit, a roof unit, and a cupola unit as shown. Join the pieces to make a Pinwheel Barn block. The block should measure 8½" × 10½". Repeat to make a light pink Pinwheel Barn block.

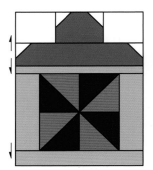 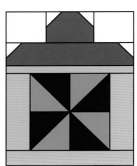

Make 1 Pinwheel Barn block of each colorway,
8½" × 10½".

4 Layer a marked white 1½" square on each end of a charcoal 2" × 8½" rectangle, right sides together as shown. Stitch, trim, and press as before to make a roof unit. Repeat to make a total of two roof units.

Make 2 units,
2" × 8½".

5 Layer marked white 1½" squares on the top corners of a charcoal 2½" × 3½" rectangle. Stitch, trim, and press as before. Make two.

Make 2 units,
2½" × 3½".

Make the Star Barn Block

1 Draw a diagonal line from corner to corner on the wrong side of each navy 1¾" square. Layer a marked square on one end of an aqua 1¾" × 3" rectangle, right sides together. Stitch on the line. Trim ¼" from the stitching line and press. Repeat on the opposite end of the rectangle to make a flying-geese unit. Repeat to make a total of four flying-geese units.

Make 4 units,
1¾" × 3".

2 Lay out the bright pink 3" square, the flying-geese units, and the aqua 1¾" squares as shown. Sew the units together in each row. Join the rows to make the star unit. The unit should measure 5½" square.

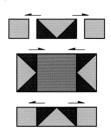
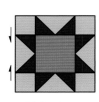

Make 1 unit,
5½" × 5½".

3 Sew the blue 2" × 5½" strips to the sides of the star. Sew the blue 1" × 8½" strip to the top of the unit and the aqua 1½" × 8½" strip to the bottom to make a barn unit. The barn unit should measure 7" × 8½".

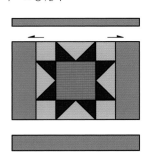
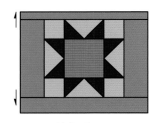

Make 1 unit,
7" × 8½".

4 Sew the white A and A reversed triangles to the charcoal B roof piece to make a roof unit.

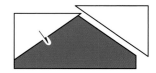

Make 1 unit,
4" × 8½".

5 Stitch the roof unit to the barn unit to make the Star Barn block. The block should measure 8½" × 10½".

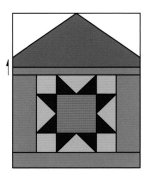

Make 1 Star Barn block,
8½" × 10½".

Assemble the Row

Lay out the blocks and white 1½" × 10½" strips in alternating positions. Join the blocks and strips into a row, and press the seam allowances toward the strips. The completed row should measure 10½" × 48½", including seam allowances.

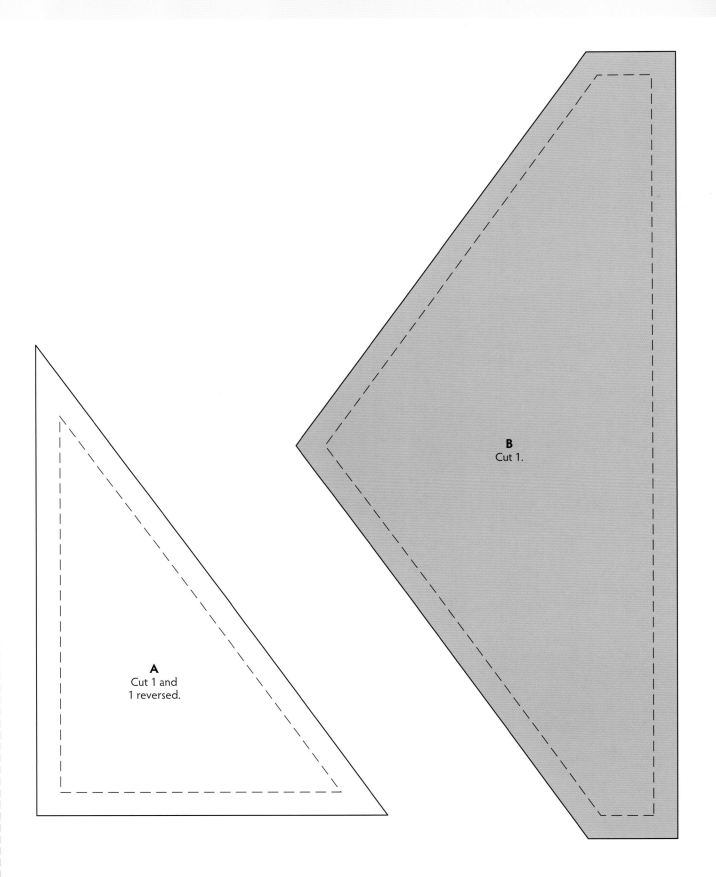

A
Cut 1 and
1 reversed.

B
Cut 1.

Little Beach Houses

Designed by **KARLA EISENACH** of Sweetwater

FINISHED ROW: 8" × 48"

Ah, a day at the beach—little beach huts with pennants flapping in the ocean breeze—this is the next best thing to being there.

Materials

Yardage is based on 42"-wide fabric.

⅜ yard of cream print for background
6" × 6" square *each of 5* assorted black prints for houses
3½" × 6½" rectangle *each of 5* assorted red prints for roofs
2½" × 4½" rectangle *each of 5* assorted cream-and-red prints for doors
2½" × 2½" square *each of 12* assorted red prints for flag appliqués
⅛ yard of 17"-wide lightweight paper-backed fusible web
Black pearl cotton or embroidery floss

Cutting

All measurements include ¼"-wide seam allowances.

From the cream print, cut:

1 strip, 8½" × 42"; crosscut into:
    4 rectangles, 4½" × 8½"
    2 rectangles, 1½" × 8½"
    10 rectangles, 1" × 5½"
1 strip, 3½" × 42"; crosscut into 10 squares, 3½" × 3½"

From *each of the 5* black prints cut:

2 rectangles, 2" × 5½" (10 total)
1 rectangle, 1½" × 2½" (5 total)

Make the Blocks

Press all seam allowances as indicated by the arrows, or as otherwise instructed.

1 Lay out two matching black 2" × 5½" rectangles and one 1½" × 2½" rectangle, one door rectangle, and two cream 1" × 5½" rectangles as shown. Sew the pieces together to make a house unit. The house unit should measure 5½" × 6½". Repeat to make a total of five house units.

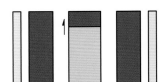 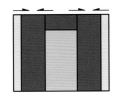

Make 5 units,
5½" × 6½".

2 Draw a diagonal line from corner to corner on the wrong side of each cream 3½" square. Layer a marked square on one end of a red print rectangle, right sides together as shown. Stitch on the marked line. Trim ¼" from the stitching line. Layer another marked square on the opposite end of

the rectangle as shown; stitch, trim, and press as before to make a roof unit. The roof unit should measure 3½" × 6½". Repeat to make a total of five roof units.

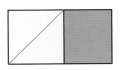 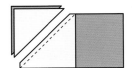

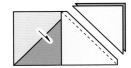 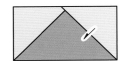

Make 5 units,
3½" × 6½".

3 Sew a roof unit to the top of a house unit to make a House block. The block should measure 6½" × 8½". Repeat to make a total of five House blocks.

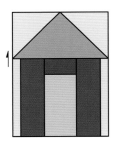

Make 5 blocks,
6½" × 8½".

Assemble the Row

Lay out the blocks and remaining cream rectangles in alternating positions. Join the pieces into a row and press the seam allowances toward the rectangles. The completed row should measure 8½" × 48½", including seam allowances.

Appliqué the Row

For information on appliqué and embroidery techniques, go to ShopMartingale.com/HowtoQuilt.

1 Using the flag pattern below, prepare 12 flags for fusible appliqué. Referring to the photo on page 75, position the flags on the background. Follow the manufacturer's instructions to fuse the flags in place.

2 Using black pearl cotton or two strands of black embroidery floss, stitch around each appliqué with a blanket stitch. Connect the flags to each other and to the houses with a backstitch.

Appliqué pattern does not include seam allowances.

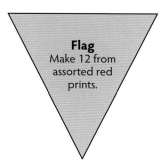

Flag
Make 12 from assorted red prints.

Color Wheels

Designed by **CAMILLE ROSKELLEY** of Thimble Blossoms

FINISHED ROW: 11¼" × 48"

These blocks start out as pinwheels, but a quick diagonal-seam piecing method transforms them into wheels.

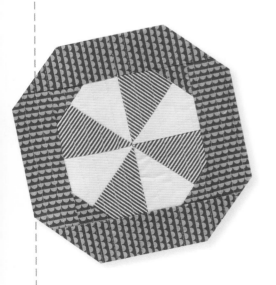

Materials

Yardage is based on 42"-wide fabric. Fat eighths are 9" × 21".

⅝ yard of white solid for background and border

1 fat eighth *each of 10* assorted prints (2 aqua, 2 green, 2 pink, 2 red, 2 blue) for blocks

Cutting

All measurements include ¼"-wide seam allowances.

From the white solid, cut:

1 strip, 3½" × 42"; crosscut into 10 squares, 3½" × 3½"

2 strips, 2½" × 42"; crosscut into 20 squares, 2½" × 2½"

3 strips, 1¾" × 42"; crosscut into:

    5 strips, 1¾" × 9¾"

    5 strips, 1¾" × 8½"

3 strips, 1½" × 42"

1 strip, 2" × 9¾"

1 strip, ¾" × 9¾"

From one fat eighth of *each* color, cut:

2 squares, 3½" × 3½" (10 total)

From the second fat eighth of *each* color, cut:

2 strips, 2" × 8½" (10 total)

2 strips, 2" × 5½" (10 total)

4 squares, 1¾" × 1¾" (20 total)

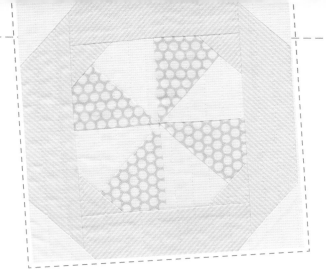

Make the Blocks

Press all seam allowances as indicated by the arrows, or as otherwise instructed.

1 Draw a diagonal line from corner to corner on the wrong side of each white 3½" square.

2 Layer a marked square on an aqua 3½" square, right sides together. Stitch ¼" from both sides of the marked line. Cut the square on the line to make two half-square-triangle units. Repeat with the matching aqua square to make a total of four half-square-triangle units. Trim each unit to 3" square.

Make 4.

3 Lay out the half-square-triangle units in two rows of two as shown. Sew the units together in each row. Join the rows to make a pinwheel unit. The pinwheel unit should measure 5½" square.

Make 1 unit,
5½" × 5½".

4 Draw a diagonal line from corner to corner on the wrong side of each aqua 1¾" square. Layer the marked squares on the pinwheel unit, right sides together as shown. Stitch on the marked lines. Trim ¼" from the stitching lines.

Make 1 unit,
5½" × 5½".

5 Sew the aqua 2" × 5½" strips to the sides of the pinwheel unit. Sew the aqua 2" × 8½" strips to the top and bottom of the unit. The unit should now measure 8½" square.

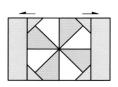 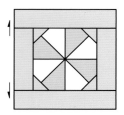

Make 1 unit,
8½" × 8½".

6 Draw a diagonal line from corner to corner on the wrong side of each white 2½" square. Layer four marked squares on the pinwheel unit, right sides together as shown. Stitch on the marked lines. Trim ¼" from the stitching lines to make a Wheel block.

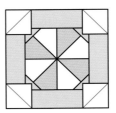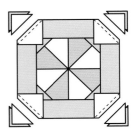

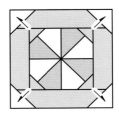

Make 1 block,
8½" × 8½".

7 Sew a white 1¾" × 8½" strip to the left edge of the Wheel block. Sew a white 1¾" × 9¾" strip to the top edge of the block. The bordered block should measure 9¾" square.

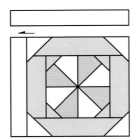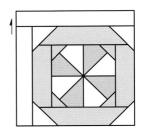

Make 1 bordered block,
9¾" × 9¾".

8 Repeat steps 2–7 to make a total of five bordered blocks.

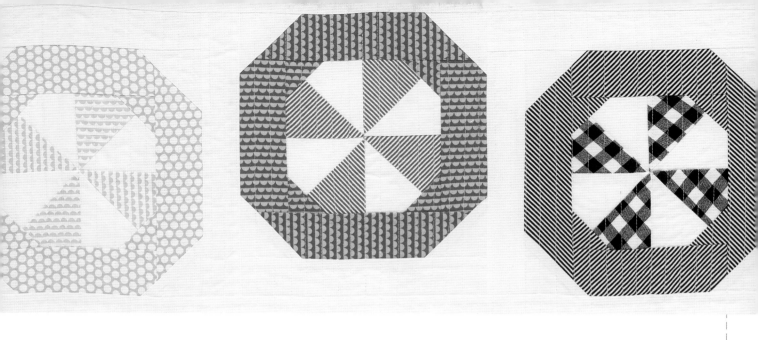

Assemble the Row

1 Lay out the bordered blocks side by side in a horizontal row, rotating them as shown. Join the blocks and press the seam allowances as indicated. Sew the white 2" × 9¾" strip to the right end of the row and the white ¾" × 9¾" strip to the left end.

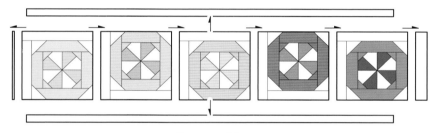

Row assembly

2 Piece the white 1½"-wide strips together end to end. From the pieced strip, cut two strips, 48½" long. Sew the strips to the top and bottom of the row. Press the seam allowances toward the strips. The completed row should measure 11¾" × 48½", including seam allowances.

Stars in Bloom

Designed by **SHERRI MCCONNELL**

FINISHED ROW: 8" × 48"

Traditional Star blocks are always a favorite. Make yours scrappy or with two prints in each block like the ones shown here.

Materials

Yardage is based on 42"-wide fabric.

½ yard of white solid for background
10" × 10" square *each of 6* assorted prints for triangles
5" × 5" square *each of 6* assorted prints for rectangles

Cutting

All measurements include ¼"-wide seam allowances.

From the white solid, cut:
3 strips, 2⅝" × 42"; crosscut into 36 squares, 2⅝" × 2⅝"
2 strips, 2⅛" × 42"; crosscut into 24 squares, 2⅛" × 2⅛"
2 strips, 2" × 42"; crosscut into:
    24 rectangles, 2" × 2⅛"
    6 squares, 2" × 2"

From *each* print 10" square, cut:
6 squares, 2⅝" × 2⅝" (36 total)

From *each* print 5" square, cut:
4 rectangles, 2" × 2⅛" (24 total)

Make the Blocks

Press all seam allowances as indicated by the arrows, or as otherwise instructed.

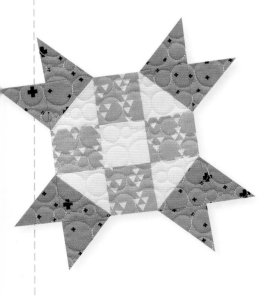

1 Draw a diagonal line from corner to corner on the wrong side of each white 2⅝" square. Layer a marked square on a print 2⅝" square, right sides together. Stitch ¼" from both sides of the marked line. Cut

the squares on the line to make two half-square-triangle units. Trim each unit to 2⅛" square. Repeat to make 12 matching half-square-triangle units.

Make 12 units.

2 Join four white 2⅛" squares, the half-square-triangle units, four white 2" × 2⅛" rectangles, four matching 2" × 2⅛" rectangles, and one white 2" square in five rows of five as shown.

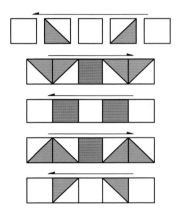

3 Join the rows to make a block. The block should measure 8½" square.

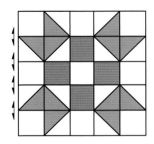

Make 1 block, 8½" × 8½".

4 Repeat steps 1–3 to make a total of six blocks.

Assemble the Row

Join the blocks, turning every other block so seams nest. Press seam allowances open. The row should measure 8½" × 48½", including seam allowances.

Tricolor Stars

Designed by **LISA BONGEAN of Primitive Gatherings**

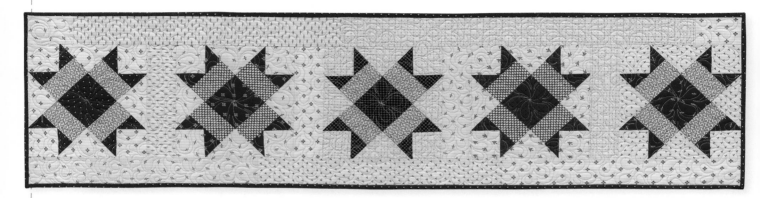

FINISHED ROW: 11¼" × 48"

Classic stars are perfect in any setting and in any color. Whether you make them red like these or choose your favorite color, you can't miss.

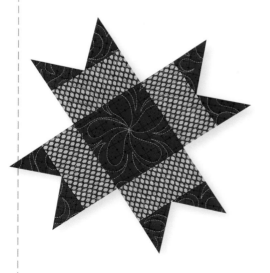

Materials

Yardage is based on 42"-wide fabric. Fat quarters are 18" × 21".

10" × 10" square *each of 5* assorted dark red prints for blocks

10" × 10" square *each of 5* assorted light red prints for blocks

1 fat quarter *each of 5* assorted light tan prints for background and border

Cutting

All measurements include ¼"-wide seam allowances.

From *each of the* 5 dark red prints, cut:

1 square, 3½" × 3½" (5 total)

4 squares, 2⅜" × 2⅜"; cut the squares in half diagonally to yield 8 triangles (40 total)

From *each of the* 5 light red prints, cut:

4 rectangles, 2" × 3½" (20 total)

From *each of the* 5 light tan prints, cut:

1 square, 5½" × 5½"; cut the square into quarters diagonally to yield 4 triangles (20 total)

4 squares, 2⅝" × 2⅝" (20 total)

From the remainder of light tan prints, cut a *total* of:

8 strips, 1⅞" × 21"; from *each of 4* of the strips, cut 1 sashing strip, 1⅞" × 9" (4 total)

Make the Blocks

Press all seam allowances as indicated by the arrows, or as otherwise instructed.

1 Sew two matching dark red print triangles to one tan print square as shown. Repeat to make a total of four matching units.

Make 4 units.

2 Sew a light red rectangle to a unit from step 1 to make a corner unit. Make four matching units.

Make 4 units.

3 Join the corner units, matching dark red print square, and four matching light triangles in three diagonal rows as shown. Join the rows to make a block. The block should measure 9" square.

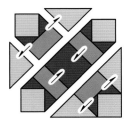 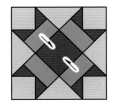

Make 1 block,
9" × 9".

4 Repeat steps 1–3 to make a total of five blocks.

Assemble the Row

1 Sew the blocks and sashing strips together in alternating positions.

2 Join the remaining tan 1⅞"-wide strips to make two 48½"-long borders. Sew to the top and bottom of the row. Press the seam allowances toward the strips. The row should measure 11¾" × 48½", including seam allowances.

Stars and Geese

Designed by **BETSY CHUTCHIAN of Betsy's Best Quilts and More**

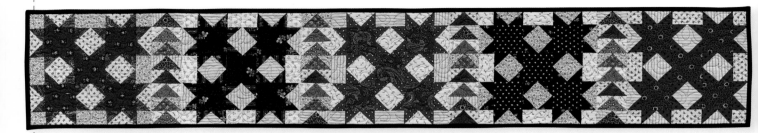

FINISHED ROW: 8" × 48"

What's better than one traditional design? Two! These Star blocks and flying geese are made with reproduction prints for a vintage look.

Materials

Fat eighths are 9" × 21".

1 fat eighth *each of 5* light prints for blocks and sashing
10" × 10" square *each of 4* assorted navy prints for blocks
10" × 10" square *each of 6* assorted red prints for blocks
5" × 5" square *each of 8* assorted green prints for sashing

Cutting

All measurements include ¼"-wide seam allowances.

From *each of the 5* light prints, cut:
4 squares, 2½" × 2½" (20 total)
12 rectangles, 1½" × 2½" (60 total)
18 squares, 1½" × 1½" (90 total)

From *each of 2* navy prints, cut:
5 squares, 2½" × 2½" (10 total)

From *each of the 2* remaining navy prints, cut:
32 squares, 1½" × 1½" (64 total)

From *each of 3* red prints, cut:
5 squares, 2½" × 2½" (15 total)

From *each of the 3* remaining red prints, cut:
32 squares, 1½" × 1½" (96 total)

From *each of the 8* green prints, cut:
4 rectangles, 1½" × 2½" (32 total)

Make the Star Blocks

Press all seam allowances as indicated by the arrows, or as otherwise instructed.

1 Separate the light print pieces into five block groups. Each group should have four 2½" squares and eight 1½" × 2½" rectangles in one print, and four 1½" × 2½" rectangles and four 1½" squares in a different print. Save the remaining 1½" squares for the flying-geese units. For steps 2–6, use pieces from one block group.

2 Draw a diagonal line from corner to corner on the wrong side of each navy 1½" square. Layer two matching marked squares on opposite corners of a light 2½" square, right sides together. Stitch on the marked lines as shown. Trim ¼" from the stitching lines. Press the seam allowances toward the corners. Repeat with matching navy squares for the remaining corners to make a navy square-in-a-square unit. Repeat to make a total of four matching navy square-in-a-square units.

Make 4 units,
2½" × 2½".

3 Place a matching marked navy square on one end of a light 1½" × 2½" rectangle, right sides together. Stitch on the marked line. Trim ¼" from the stitching line. Repeat for the opposite end to make a star-point unit. Repeat to make a total of eight matching star-point units.

Make 8 units,
1½" × 2½".

4 Lay out one navy 2½" square, two star-point units, and one light 1½" square as shown. Sew the pieces into two rows. Join the rows to make a corner unit. The unit should be 3½" square. Repeat to make a total of four matching corner units.

Make 4 units,
3½" × 3½".

5 Sew a light 1½" × 2½" rectangle to each square-in-a-square unit to make a side unit. Repeat to make a total of four side units.

Make 4 units,
2½" × 3½".

HERE'S THE SKINNY ON
BETSY CHUTCHIAN

Everything old is new again when Betsy gets involved. A lover of all things 19th century, she's making classics for a new generation (BetsysBestQuiltsandMore.blogspot.com).

I'm currently obsessed with Netflix. I watch/listen while I sew.

I'd line up every time to eat on the patio at Joe T. Garcia's in Fort Worth, Texas.

My go-to sewing thread color is Aurifil #2326 soft tan/light brown. I use it for 95% of my piecing.

My most-productive time of day to sew is 1:00 to 3:00 p.m.

My favorite marking tool is a Sewline white mechanical pencil. I use it for appliqué or my simple machine quilting.

The last great series I binge-watched was *The Crown*, then *Stranger Things*, literally one after the other, not continuously around the clock, but successively, LOL.

My go-to rotary cutter is a 28 mm.

My go-to scissors are Kai brand in different sizes, but the little curved blade and bent handle snips are fabulous at the sewing machine!

When pulling fabric for a single row like this, I begin by looking at my stash by colors and then decide on a pleasing combination.

One little tip that will make creating my row better is: Pre-starch and press all fabrics before cutting and sewing.

6 Lay out the corner units, matching navy 2½" square, and side units in three rows of three as shown. Sew the pieces together in each row. Join the rows to complete a Star block. The block should be 8½" square.

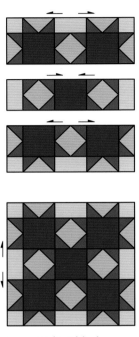

Make 1 block,
8½" × 8½".

7 Repeat steps 2–6 to make a second navy block and three red blocks.

Make the Flying-Geese Units

1 Draw a diagonal line from corner to corner on the wrong side of each of 64 light 1½" squares (you will have six light squares left over). Place a marked square on one end of a green 1½" × 2½" rectangle, right sides together. Stitch on the marked line. Trim ¼" from the stitching line. Press the seam allowances toward the corner. Repeat for the opposite end with a matching light square to make a flying-geese unit. Repeat to make a total of 32 flying-geese units.

Make 32 units,
1½" × 2½".

2 Lay out eight flying-geese units in a vertical row as shown. Join the units to make a sashing row. Press the seam allowances toward the bottom. Repeat to make a total of four sashing rows. The rows should measure 2½" × 8½".

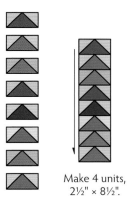

Make 4 units,
2½" × 8½".

Assemble the Row

Lay out the blocks and sashing rows in alternating positions. Join the blocks and rows, and press the seam allowances open. The completed row should measure 8½" × 48½", including seam allowances.

Evening Stars

Designed by JO MORTON

FINISHED ROW: 9⅛" × 48"

Variable Star blocks are timeless, and even better, they're easy to make. Set on point, they make a dramatic display.

Materials

Yardage is based on 42"-wide fabric. Fat quarters are 18"×21".

5" × 5" square *each of 13* assorted brown prints for star points
7" × 7" square *each of 13* assorted light prints for blocks
⅓ yard of teal print for sashing
10" × 10" square of brown print for cornerstones
1 fat quarter of pink print for setting triangles

Cutting

All measurements include ¼"-wide seam allowances.

From *each of the 13* brown prints, cut:
4 squares, 1⅞" × 1⅞" (52 total)

From *each of the 13* light prints, cut:
1 square, 3¼" × 3¼" (13 total)
1 square, 2½" × 2½" (13 total)
4 squares, 1½" × 1½" (52 total)

From the teal print, cut:
2 strips, 4½" × 42"; crosscut into 42 strips, 1½" × 4½"

From the brown print, cut:
13 squares, 1½" × 1½"

From the pink print, cut:
4 squares, 6" × 6"; cut the squares into quarters diagonally to yield 16 triangles (1 is extra)
1 square, 4" × 4"; cut the square in half diagonally to yield 2 triangles

Make the Blocks

Press all seam allowances as indicated by the arrows, or as otherwise instructed.

1 Draw a diagonal line from corner to corner on the wrong side of four matching brown 1⅞" squares. Lay two marked squares on a light print 3¼" square, right sides together as shown. Stitch ¼" from the line on both sides. Cut on the line.

2 Place a marked brown square on the corner of one unit from step 1, aligning the edges as shown. Stitch ¼" from the line on both sides. Cut on the line to yield two flying-geese units. Each flying-geese unit should measure 1½" × 2½". Repeat for the remaining unit.

Make 4 units,
1½" × 2½".

3 Lay out one light 2½" square, the flying-geese units, and four matching light 1½" squares as shown. Sew the pieces together in each row. Join the rows to make a Star block. The block should measure 4½" square. Repeat to make a total of 13 blocks.

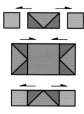

Make 13 blocks,
4½" × 4½".

Assemble the Row

1 Lay out the blocks, teal strips, brown squares, 15 pink quarter-square triangles, and two pink half-square triangles as shown. Sew the pieces into diagonal rows. The setting triangles were cut oversized and will be trimmed in the final step. Press the seam allowances toward the teal sashing, or refer to "Jo's Clipping Trick" to reduce bulk in the seams.

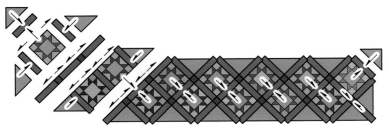

Row assembly

2 Join the rows. Press the seam allowances toward the teal sashing.

3 Place the ¼" line of a ruler on the outer points of the blocks. Trim along the edge of the ruler to straighten the edges, leaving a ¼" seam allowance. The completed row should measure 9⅝" × 48½", including seam allowances.

Align ¼" mark on ruler with block point. Trim.

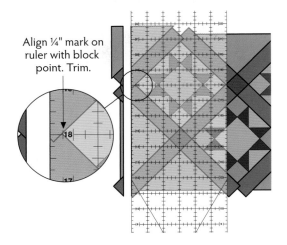

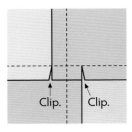
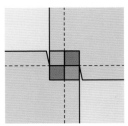

Blender Rows

Designed by **LISSA ALEXANDER of ModaLissa**

When deciding which rows you want to make for your row quilts, consider a few of these spacer or blender rows for fun and interest. Or, make a quilt using just blender rows, a quilt using your favorite row repeated in different colors, or in just one color with one background for a two-color quilt. You can sew the rows into a vertical layout for a baby quilt or throw—there are so many possibilities!

Join Hands

FINISHED ROW: 4" × 48"

Materials

Fat eighths are 9" × 21".

10" × 10" square *each of 6 assorted light fabrics* (or 1 fat eighth)

10" × 10" square *each of 6 assorted dark fabrics* (or 1 fat eighth)

Cutting

All measurements include ¼"-wide seam allowances.

From *each of the 6* light fabrics, cut:

1 square, 2½" × 2½" (6 total)
4 rectangles, 1½" × 2" (24 total)
4 squares, 1½" × 1½" (24 total)
4 rectangles, 1" × 1½" (24 total)

From *each of the 6* dark fabrics, cut:

1 square, 2½" × 2½" (6 total)
4 rectangles, 1½" × 2" (24 total)
4 squares, 1½" × 1½" (24 total)
4 rectangles, 1" × 1½" (24 total)

Make the Blocks

1 Join two matching dark 1½" × 2" rectangles and one light 1½" square as shown to make a long side unit. Repeat to make a total of two long side units.

Make 2 units,
1½" × 4½".

2 Using same fabrics as in step 1, join two dark 1" × 1½" rectangles and one light 1½" square as shown to make a short side unit. Repeat to make a total of two short side units.

Make 2 units,
1½" × 2½".

3 Join short side units to opposite edges of a matching light 2½" square. Sew long side units as shown to make a dark block. The block should measure 4½" square.

Make 1 block,
4½" × 4½".

4 Repeat steps 1–3 to make a total of six dark blocks.

5 Reversing placement of lights and darks, repeat steps 1–3 to make six light blocks; press the seam allowances in opposite direction in steps 2 and 3.

Make 6 blocks,
4½" × 4½".

Assemble the Row

Lay out the blocks side by side in one horizontal row, alternating light and dark blocks. Join the blocks and press the seam allowances toward the dark blocks. The completed row should measure 4½" × 48½", including seam allowances.

Floral Frenzy

FINISHED ROW: 4" × 48"

Materials

Fat quarters are 18" × 21".

5" × 5" square *each of 12* assorted light fabrics
   (or 1 fat quarter)
3½" × 6" rectangle *each of 12* assorted dark fabrics
   (or 1 fat quarter)
1½" × 1½" square *each of 12* assorted medium
   fabrics (or 1 square, 10" × 10")

Cutting

All measurements include ¼"-wide seam allowances.

From *each of the 12* light fabrics, cut:
1 square, 3" × 3" (12 total)
1 rectangle, 1½" × 2½" (12 total)
1 square, 1½" × 1½" (12 total)

From *each of the 12* dark fabrics, cut:
1 square, 3" × 3" (12 total)
1 square, 2½" × 2½" (12 total)

Make the Blocks

1 Draw a diagonal line from corner to corner on the wrong side of each light 3" square. Layer a marked square on a dark 3" square, right sides together. Stitch ¼" from both sides of the marked line. Cut the squares on the line to make two half-square-triangle units. Press the seam allowances toward the dark prints. Repeat to make 12 pairs of matching half-square-triangle units. Trim each unit to 2½" square.

Make 24 units.

2 Join a light 1½" square and a medium 1½" square. Sew a matching light 1½" × 2½" rectangle to the unit as shown to make a bud unit. Repeat to make a total of 12 bud units.

Make 12 units,
2½" × 2½".

3 Matching the light prints and dark prints, lay out two half-square-triangle units, one bud unit, and one dark 2½" square as shown in two rows. Sew the pieces in each row together. Join the rows to make a block, which should measure 4½" square. Repeat to make a total of 12 blocks.

Make 12 blocks,
4½" × 4½".

Assemble the Row

Lay out the blocks side by side in one horizontal row. Join the blocks and press the seam allowances open. The completed row should measure 4½" × 48½", including seam allowances.

Stair Steps

FINISHED ROW: 4½" × 48"

Materials

Yardage is based on 42"-wide fabric.

¼ yard of light fabric

¼ yard of dark fabric

Cutting

All measurements include ¼"-wide seam allowances.

From the light fabric, cut:

3 strips, 2" × 42"; crosscut into:
   16 rectangles, 2" × 3½"
   16 squares, 2" × 2"

From the dark fabric, cut:

3 strips, 2" × 42"; crosscut into 24 rectangles,
   2" × 3½"

Make the Blocks

Lay out two light 2" × 3½" rectangles, two light 2" squares, and three dark 2" × 3½" rectangles as shown. Sew the pieces together in each row. Join the rows to make a block. Repeat to make a total of eight blocks. Press the seam allowances toward the middle row on four blocks and toward the top and bottom row on four blocks. Each block should be 6½" × 5".

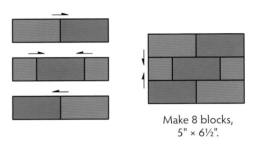

Make 8 blocks,
5" × 6½".

Assemble the Row

Lay out the blocks side by side in one horizontal row, alternating the direction of the seams. Join the blocks. Press the seam allowances open. The completed row should measure 5" × 48½", including seam allowances.

Combine Stars in Bloom (page 88) with two Scallops rows (opposite).

Scallops

FINISHED ROW: 2" × 48"

Materials

Yardage is based on 42"-wide fabric. Fat eighths are 9" × 21".

¼ yard of light fabric for background
1 fat eighth of dark fabric for appliqués

Cutting

All measurements include ¼"-wide seam allowances.

From the light fabric, cut:
2 strips, 2½" × 42"

Appliqué the Row

1 Piece the 2½"-wide light strips end to end to make one 48½"-long strip.

2 Using the pattern at right, prepare the scallops for fusible appliqué. For illustrated information on fusible appliqué, go to ShopMartingale.com/HowtoQuilt.

3 Arrange the scallops on the pieced light strip, leaving ¼" seam allowances at both ends of the strip as shown below. Follow the manufacturer's instructions to fuse the shapes in place.

4 Stitch around the curved edges of the scallop appliqués with a zigzag stitch. The completed row should measure 2½" × 48½", including seam allowances.

¼"   Row assembly   ¼"

Scallop
Make 6.

¼" seam allowance

Criss Cross

FINISHED ROW: 4" × 48"

Materials

Fat quarters are 18" × 21".

10" × 10" square *each of 6* assorted light fabrics
(or 1 fat quarter)
10" × 10" square *each of 6* assorted dark fabrics
(or 1 fat quarter)

Cutting

All measurements include ¼"-wide seam allowances.

From *each of the 6* light fabrics, cut:
4 squares, 2¼" × 2¼" (24 total)
1 rectangle, 1" × 4½" (6 total)
2 rectangles, 1" × 2¼" (12 total)

From *each of the 6* dark fabrics, cut:
4 squares, 2¼" × 2¼" (24 total)
1 rectangle, 1" × 4½" (6 total)
2 rectangles, 1" × 2¼" (12 total)

Make the Blocks

1 Lay out two light 1" × 2¼" rectangles, one light 1" × 4½" rectangle, and four dark 2¼" squares as shown. Sew the pieces together in each row. Join the rows and light rectangle to make a dark block. The block should measure 4½" square. Repeat to make a total of six dark blocks.

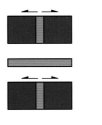

Make 6 blocks,
4½" × 4½".

2 Lay out two dark 1" × 2¼" rectangles, one dark 1" × 4½" rectangle, and four light 2¼" squares as shown. Sew the pieces together in each row. Join the rows and dark rectangle to make a light block. The block should measure 4½" square. Repeat to make a total of six light blocks.

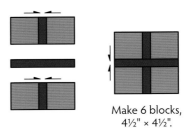

Make 6 blocks,
4½" × 4½".

Assemble the Row

Lay out the blocks side by side in one horizontal row, alternating light and dark blocks. Join the blocks and press the seam allowances toward the dark blocks. The completed row should measure 4½" × 48½", including seam allowances.

Looking Glass

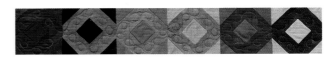

FINISHED ROW: 4" × 48"

Materials

Yardage is based on 42"-wide fabric.

10" × 10" square *each of 6* assorted light fabrics
(or ⅓ yard)
10" × 10" square *each of 6* assorted dark fabrics
(or ⅓ yard)

Cutting

All measurements include ¼"-wide seam allowances.

From *each of the* 6 light fabrics, cut:
2 rectangles, 1½" × 4½" (12 total)
2 rectangles, 1½" × 2½" (12 total)
1 square, 2½" × 2½" (6 total)
4 squares, 2" × 2" (24 total)
4 squares, 1½" × 1½" (24 total)

From *each of the* 6 dark fabrics, cut:
2 rectangles, 1½" × 4½" (12 total)
2 rectangles, 1½" × 2½" (12 total)
1 square, 2½" × 2½" (6 total)
4 squares, 2" × 2" (24 total)
4 squares, 1½" × 1½" (24 total)

Make the Blocks

1 Draw a diagonal line from corner to corner on the wrong side of each dark and light 1½" square and each dark and light 2" square.

2 Layer a marked light 1½" square on one corner of a dark 2½" square, right sides together. Stitch on the marked line. Trim ¼" from the stitching line. Repeat on the remaining corners with matching light print squares to make a dark center unit.

Make 1 unit,
2½" × 2½".

3 Sew two matching light 1½" × 2½" rectangles to opposite edges of a dark center unit. Sew two matching light 1½" × 4½" rectangles to the remaining edges of the unit.

Make 1 unit,
4½" × 4½".

4 Layer a marked dark 2" square on one corner of the unit from step 3, right sides together. Stitch, trim, and press as before. Repeat on the remaining corners with matching dark print squares to make a light block, which should be 4½" square.

Make 6 blocks,
4½" × 4½".

5 Repeat steps 2–4 to make a total of six light blocks.

6 Reversing placement of lights and darks, repeat steps 2–4 to make six dark blocks.

Make 6 blocks,
4½" × 4½".

Assemble the Row

Lay out the blocks side by side in one horizontal row, alternating dark and light blocks. Join the blocks and press the seam allowances open. The completed row should measure 4½" × 48½", including seam allowances.

Twigs

FINISHED ROW: 4" × 48"

Materials

Fat quarters are 18" × 21". Fat eighths are 9" × 21".

5" × 5" square *each of 12* assorted dark fabrics
(or 1 fat eighth)

5" × 5" square *each of 12* assorted medium fabrics
(or 1 fat eighth)

5" × 5" square *each of 12* assorted light fabrics
(or 1 fat quarter)

Cutting

All measurements include ¼"-wide seam allowances.

From *each of the 12* dark fabrics, cut:
2 rectangles, 1" × 2½" (24 total)
2 rectangles, 1" × 2" (24 total)

From *each of the 12* medium fabrics, cut:
2 rectangles, 1" × 2½" (24 total)
2 rectangles, 1" × 2" (24 total)

From *each of the 12* light fabrics, cut:
4 squares, 2" × 2" (48 total)

Make the Blocks

1 Sew a dark 1" × 2" rectangle to a light 2" square as shown. Sew a matching 1" × 2½" dark rectangle to the unit. Repeat to make a total of two matching dark units and two medium units with the same light print.

Make 2 units,   Make 2 units,
2½" × 2½".   2½" × 2½".

2 Repeat step 1 to make a total of 24 dark units and 24 medium units (12 sets of two matching dark units and two matching medium units).

3 Lay out two matching dark units and two matching medium units in two rows as shown. Join the units in each row. Join the rows to make a block. The block should measure 4½" square. Repeat to make a total of 12 blocks.

Make 12 blocks,
4½" × 4½".

Assemble the Row

Lay out the blocks side by side in one horizontal row, rotating every other block 180° so the seams abut. Join the blocks and press the seam allowances in one direction. The completed row should measure 4½" × 48½", including seam allowances.

Beans

FINISHED ROW: 4" × 48"

Materials

Fat quarters are 18" × 21".

10" × 10" square (or 1 fat quarter) *each of 6* assorted dark fabrics for background

10" × 10" square (or 1 fat quarter) *each of 6* assorted light fabrics for background

2½" × 4½" rectangle *each of 12* assorted bright fabrics for beans

Cutting

All measurements include ¼"-wide seam allowances.

From *each of the 6* dark fabrics, cut:
2 rectangles, 1½" × 4½" (12 total)
4 squares, 1½" × 1½" (24 total)

From *each of the 6* light fabrics, cut:
2 rectangles, 1½" × 4½" (12 total)
4 squares, 1½" × 1½" (24 total)

Make the Blocks

1 Draw a diagonal line from corner to corner on the wrong side of each light 1½" square and each dark 1½" square.

2 Layer two marked matching light squares on opposite corners of a bright 2½" × 4½" rectangle, right sides together. Stitch on the marked lines. Trim ¼" from the stitching lines. Repeat on the remaining corners with matching light squares.

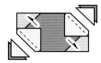

Make 1 unit,
2½" × 4½".

3 Sew two matching light 1½" × 4½" rectangles to the unit from step 2 as shown to make a light block. The block should measure 4½" square.

Make 1 block,
4½" × 4½".

4 Repeat steps 2 and 3 to make a total of six light blocks.

5 Using dark and bright fabrics, repeat steps 2–4 to make six dark blocks. Press seam allowances in the opposite direction from step 3.

Make 6 blocks,
4½" × 4½".

Assemble the Row

Lay out the blocks side by side in one horizontal row, alternating light and dark backgrounds. Join the blocks and press the seam allowances toward the dark blocks. The completed row should measure 4½" × 48½", including seam allowances.

Silly Row

FINISHED ROW: 4" × 48"

Materials

Yardage is based on 42"-wide fabric. Fat quarters are 18" × 21".

10" × 10" square *each of 12* assorted light fabrics (or ⅜ yard)

5" × 5" square *each of 12* assorted medium fabrics (or 1 fat quarter)

5" × 5" square *each of 12* assorted dark fabrics (or ⅓ yard)

Cutting

All measurements include ¼"-wide seam allowances.

From *each of the 12* light fabrics, cut:
4 rectangles, 1" × 2½" (48 total)
4 squares, 2" × 2" (48 total)
4 rectangles, 1" × 2" (48 total)

From *each of the 12* medium fabrics, cut:
4 squares, 2" × 2" (48 total)

From *each of the 12* dark fabrics, cut:
4 squares, 2½" × 2½" (48 total)

Make the Blocks

1 Join a dark square and a light 1" × 2" rectangle as shown. Sew a light 1" × 2½" rectangle to the bottom of the unit. Repeat to make a total of four matching units.

Make 4 units,
2½" × 2½".

2 Draw a diagonal line from corner to corner on the wrong side of each light 2" square from the same light print used in step 1. Layer a marked light square on a unit from step 1, right sides together. Stitch on the marked line. Trim ¼" from the stitching line. Repeat with all units from step 1.

Make 4 units,
2½" × 2½".

3 Draw a diagonal line from corner to corner on the wrong side of four matching medium 2½" squares. Layer a marked medium square on a unit from step 2, right sides together. Stitch on the marked line. Trim ¼" from the stitching line. Repeat with all units from step 2.

Make 4 units,
2½" × 2½".

4 Lay out the units from step 3 in two rows of two as shown. Join the units in each row. Join the rows to make a block. The block should measure 4½" square.

Make 1 block,
4½" × 4½".

5 Repeat steps 1–4 to make a total of 12 blocks.

Assemble the Row

Lay out the blocks side by side in one horizontal row. Join the blocks and press the seam allowances open. The completed row should measure 4½" × 48½", including seam allowances.

Triangles

FINISHED ROW: 3½" × 48"

Materials

Yardage is based on 42"-wide fabric.

¼ yard of light fabric
¼ yard of dark fabric
Template plastic

Cutting

All measurements include ¼"-wide seam allowances. Trace the triangle pattern below onto template plastic and cut it out. Use the template to cut the triangle pieces from the fabrics indicated.

From the light fabric strip, cut:

1 strip, 4" × 42"; cut into 13 triangles (see illustration above right)

From the dark fabric strip, cut:

1 strip, 4" × 42"; cut into 12 triangles (see illustration above right)

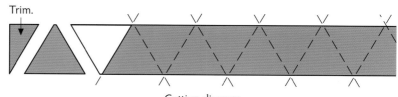

Cutting diagram
Cut 13 light triangles and 12 dark triangles.

Assemble the Row

Lay out the light and dark triangles in one horizontal row as shown. Sew the triangles together. Trim the ends of the row, leaving a ¼" seam allowance. The completed row should measure 4" × 48½", including seam allowances.

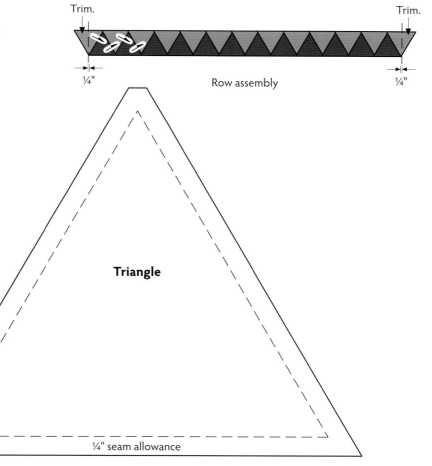

Trim.　　　　　　　　　　　　　　　Trim.

¼"　　　　　Row assembly　　　　　¼"

Triangle

¼" seam allowance

HERE'S THE SKINNY ON
LISSA ALEXANDER

She's a whiz at reinventing easier ways to piece blocks, but when you can make blender rows look anything but basic...your skills are blockbuster (ModaLissa.blogspot.com)!

I'm currently obsessed with improving my skills and precision.

I'd line up every time to go on a retreat, sewing all day and night and laughing with friends.

My go-to sewing thread color is light gray or Mother Goose (light tan).

The most productive time of day for me to sew is 9:00 to 11:00 p.m.

My favorite marking tool is a Sewline pencil.

The last great series I binge-watched was *This Is Us*. Even though this is a newer series that I watch weekly, I had to go back and watch the entire first season.

My go-to rotary cutter is a 60 mm.

My go-to scissors are Havel's 8" shears.

When pulling fabric for a single row like this, I begin by pulling a fabric that has the feel of what I envision the final project to be—lots of colors, bold and graphic, sweet and romantic. I let that fabric determine my additional fabric choices.

One little tip that will make creating my row better is this: press, don't iron. There is a difference in stretching the fabric.

Forest

FINISHED ROW: 4" × 48"

Materials

Yardage is based on 42"-wide fabric. Fat quarters are 18" × 21".

5" × 5" square *each of 12* assorted dark fabrics (or 1 fat quarter)
5" × 5" square of medium fabric for trunks
⅜ yard of light fabric for background

Cutting

All measurements include ¼"-wide seam allowances.

From *each of the 12* dark fabrics, cut:
2 rectangles, 2½" × 4½" (24 total)

From the medium fabric, cut:
12 rectangles, 1" × 1½"

From the light fabric, cut:
4 strips, 2½" × 42"; crosscut into 48 squares, 2½" × 2½"
1 strip, 2¼" × 42"; crosscut into 24 rectangles, 1½" × 2¼"

Make the Blocks

1 Draw a diagonal line from corner to corner on the wrong side of each light 2½" square. Layer a marked square on a dark rectangle, right sides together. Stitch on the marked line. Trim ¼" from the stitching line. Repeat on the opposite corner.

The unit should measure 2½" × 4½". Repeat to make a total of 24 flying-geese units.

Make 24 units,
2½" × 4½".

2 Trim ¼" off the bottom of a flying-geese unit as shown to make a treetop. Repeat to make 12 treetops, 2¼" × 4½" (one from each dark fabric).

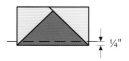

¼"

3 Trim ½" off the top of a flying-geese unit and ¼" off the bottom as shown to make a tree bottom. Repeat to make 12 tree bottoms, 1¾" × 4½".

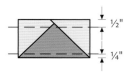

½"

¼"

4 Join a treetop and a tree bottom to make a tree unit. Notice in the quilt on page 99, the treetops and bottoms are mixed and matched. In the row at right, each tree is made with a matching top and bottom. Press the seam allowances toward the top. Repeat to make a total of 12 tree units.

Make 12 units,
3½" × 4½".

5 Join one medium 1" × 1½" rectangle and two light 1½" × 2¼" rectangles as shown to make a trunk unit. Repeat to make a total of 12 trunk units.

Make 12 units,
1½" × 4½".

6 Join a tree unit and a trunk unit to make a block that is 4½" square. Repeat to make a total of 12 blocks. Press the seam allowances toward the top of six blocks and toward the bottom of six blocks.

Make 6 of each block,
4½" × 4½".

Assemble the Row

Lay out the blocks side by side in one horizontal row. Join the blocks and press the seam allowances open. The completed row should measure 4½" × 48½", including seam allowances.

Combine Painted Ladies (page 70) with a Forest row.

Discover more fabulous quilt patterns
by your favorite Moda designers

Explore all the inspiring books in the Moda All-Stars series, where you'll discover fresh takes on classic blocks, innovative how-to tips, and clever settings that will make the fabric you love shine. Try a different technique, learn a new sewing trick, and get inspired to make a beautiful quilt today!

Find them all at your local quilt shop or online at ShopMartingale.com.

 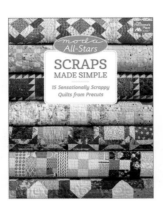